# JavaScript with Promises

D0858899

*Daniel Parker*

Beijing · Cambridge · Farnham · Köln · Sebastopol · Tokyo

**JavaScript with Promises**
by Daniel Parker

Printed in the United States of America.

Published by O'Reilly Media, Inc., 1005 Gravenstein Highway North, Sebastopol, CA 95472.

O'Reilly books may be purchased for educational, business, or sales promotional use. Online editions are also available for most titles (*http://safaribooksonline.com*). For more information, contact our corporate/institutional sales department: 800-998-9938 or corporate@oreilly.com.

| | |
|---|---|
| **Editors:** Simon St.Laurent and Brian MacDonald | **Indexer:** Wendy Catalano |
| **Production Editor:** Colleen Lobner | **Interior Designer:** David Futato |
| **Copyeditor:** Lindsy Gamble | **Cover Designer:** Ellie Volckhausen |
| **Proofreader:** Elise Morrison | **Illustrator:** Rebecca Demarest |

June 2015:          First Edition

**Revision History for the First Edition**
2015-05-28:    First Release

See *http://oreilly.com/catalog/errata.csp?isbn=9781449373214* for release details.

978-1-449-37321-4

[LSI]

# Table of Contents

# Preface

Asynchronous JavaScript is everywhere. AJAX, WebRTC, and Node.js are a few examples of where asynchronous APIs are found. Although it is easy to write a quick function to handle the result of one HTTP request, it is also easy to get lost in an unpredictable sea of callbacks as a codebase grows and more people contribute. That's where a good approach for handling asynchronous code comes in and many developers are choosing to use Promises in their approach.

This is the book I needed when originally choosing an asynchronous strategy, and it is the result of my experience using promises in JavaScript applications. It explains their use and inner workings while exposing difficulties and missteps. Promises are made up of only a few concepts with a small API. But in the same way that JavaScript's small number of simple constructs are used to create elegant and powerful solutions, I am surprised and pleased at the number of ways Promises can be used to effectively manage asynchronous code.

## Intended Audience

This book is for intermediate and advanced JavaScript developers who want to write asynchronous code. These developers may be comfortable with JavaScript for traditional web APIs but are moving to environments such as Node.js, Google Chrome packaged apps, or building desktop applications with JavaScript. Developers who write browser-based code and want to use frameworks such as Angular or newer browser technologies such as Service Workers or WebRTC will also benefit. Even people who are already experienced with Promises may still enjoy reading the code and discovering additional ideas for their own work.

## A Word on Style

This is not a book about JavaScript syntax dos and don'ts. All the examples are intended to be clear and casual; however, this style may conflict with some recommended practices. Those choices are independent of the ideas presented here and you are free to choose as you see fit when approaching these concepts in your code.

## Conventions Used in This Book

The following typographical conventions are used in this book:

*Italic*

Indicates new terms, URLs, email addresses, filenames, and file extensions.

`Constant width`

Used for program listings, as well as within paragraphs to refer to program elements such as variable or function names, databases, data types, environment variables, statements, and keywords.

**`Constant width bold`**

Shows commands or other text that should be typed literally by the user.

*`Constant width italic`*

Shows text that should be replaced with user-supplied values or by values determined by context.

This element signifies a tip or suggestion.

This element signifies a general note.

This element indicates a warning or caution.

## Using Code Examples

Supplemental material (code examples, exercises, etc.) is available for download at *https://github.com/dxparker/promises-book-examples*.

This book is here to help you get your job done. In general, if example code is offered with this book, you may use it in your programs and documentation. You do not need to contact us for permission unless you're reproducing a significant portion of the code. For example, writing a program that uses several chunks of code from this book does not require permission. Selling or distributing a CD-ROM of examples from O'Reilly books does require permission. Answering a question by citing this book and quoting example code does not require permission. Incorporating a significant amount of example code from this book into your product's documentation does require permission.

We appreciate, but do not require, attribution. An attribution usually includes the title, author, publisher, and ISBN. For example: "*JavaScript with Promises* by Daniel Parker (O'Reilly). Copyright 2015 Daniel Parker, 978-1-449-37321-4."

If you feel your use of code examples falls outside fair use or the permission given above, feel free to contact us at *permissions@oreilly.com*.

## Safari® Books Online

 *Safari Books Online* is an on-demand digital library that delivers expert content in both book and video form from the world's leading authors in technology and business.

Technology professionals, software developers, web designers, and business and creative professionals use Safari Books Online as their primary resource for research, problem solving, learning, and certification training.

Safari Books Online offers a range of plans and pricing for enterprise, government, education, and individuals.

Members have access to thousands of books, training videos, and prepublication manuscripts in one fully searchable database from publishers like O'Reilly Media, Prentice Hall Professional, Addison-Wesley Professional, Microsoft Press, Sams, Que, Peachpit Press, Focal Press, Cisco Press, John Wiley & Sons, Syngress, Morgan Kaufmann, IBM Redbooks, Packt, Adobe Press, FT Press, Apress, Manning, New Riders, McGraw-Hill, Jones & Bartlett, Course Technology, and hundreds more. For more information about Safari Books Online, please visit us online.

## How to Contact Us

Please address comments and questions concerning this book to the publisher:

O'Reilly Media, Inc.
1005 Gravenstein Highway North
Sebastopol, CA 95472
800-998-9938 (in the United States or Canada)

707-829-0515 (international or local)
707-829-0104 (fax)

We have a web page for this book, where we list errata, examples, and any additional information. You can access this page at *http://bit.ly/js-with-promises*.

To comment or ask technical questions about this book, send email to *bookquestions@oreilly.com*.

For more information about our books, courses, conferences, and news, see our website at *http://www.oreilly.com*.

Find us on Facebook: *http://facebook.com/oreilly*

Follow us on Twitter: *http://twitter.com/oreillymedia*

Watch us on YouTube: *http://www.youtube.com/oreillymedia*

## Acknowledgments

Thank you to Kris Kowal, Domenic Denicola, and Petka Antonov for their ongoing contributions to JavaScript Promises and for their feedback during the writing of this book. Thanks also to Cody Lindley for his valuable feedback.

Thank you to the wonderful people at O'Reilly whose expertise, support, and patience made the publication of this book possible, especially Simon St.Laurent for his role in getting the book started, Brian MacDonald and Amy Jollymore for their guidance, and Colleen Lobner and Lindsy Gamble for sweating the details.

One of the best things about the programming culture is constantly learning from other people or alongside them in a collaborative effort. I am grateful for having some exceptional colleagues over the years, including Jerry Raschke, Nathan Price, Hank Beasley, Gregory Long, and Johnathan Hebert.

This book is dedicated to my loving wife Sarah. You are amazing!

# CHAPTER 1

# Asynchronous JavaScript

The number of asynchronous JavaScript APIs is rapidly growing. Web applications asynchronously fetch data and load scripts in the browser. Node.js and its derivatives provide a host of APIs for asynchronous I/O. And new web specifications for Streams, Service Workers, and Font Loading all include asynchronous calls. These advancements broaden the capabilities of JavaScript applications, but using them without understanding how the async part works can result in unpredictable code that is difficult to maintain. Things may work as expected in development or test environments but fail when deployed to end users because of variables such as network speed or hardware performance.

This chapter explains how async JavaScript works. We'll cover callbacks, the event loop, and threading. Most of the information is not specific to Promises but provides the foundation you need to get the most out of Promises and out of the rest of this book.

Let's start with a code snippet that frequently surprises people. The code makes an HTTP request using the XMLHttpRequest (XHR) object and uses a `while` loop that runs for three seconds. Although it is generally bad practice to implement a delay with the `while` loop, it's a good way to illustrate how JavaScript runs. Read the code in Example 1-1 and decide whether the `listener` callback for the XHR object will ever be triggered.

*Example 1-1. Async XHR*

```
// Make an async HTTP request
var async = true;
var xhr = new XMLHttpRequest();
xhr.open('get', 'data.json', async);
xhr.send();
```

```
// Create a three second delay (don't do this in real life)
var timestamp = Date.now() + 3000;
while (Date.now() < timestamp);

// Now that three seconds have passed,
// add a listener to the xhr.load and xhr.error events
function listener() {
    console.log('greetings from listener');
}
xhr.addEventListener('load', listener);
xhr.addEventListener('error', listener);
```

Here are some common opinions on whether `listener` is called:

1. Yes, `listener` is always called

2. Not a chance, the `addEventListener` calls must run before `xhr.send()`

3. Sometimes, depending on whether the request takes more than three seconds

The correct assessment is that `listener` is always called. Although the second and third answers are common, they are incorrect because of the event loop model and run-to-completion semantics in JavaScript. If you thought otherwise or would like a refresher on these concepts, this chapter is for you.

# Callbacks

Callbacks are the cornerstone of asynchronous JavaScript programming. As a JavaScript developer you are probably familiar with callbacks, but just to be sure, Example 1-2 presents a quick case of a callback that prints each of the elements in an array.

*Example 1-2. Example callback*

```
var cities = ['Tokyo', 'London', 'Boston', 'Berlin', 'Chicago', 'New York'];

cities.forEach(function callback(city) {
    console.log(city);
});

// Console output:
// Tokyo
// London
// Boston
// Berlin
// Chicago
// New York
```

In short, a callback is a function provided to other code for invocation. Example 1-2 uses an inline function to define the callback. That is a commonly used style in Java-Script applications, but callbacks do not have to be declared inline. Example 1-3 shows the equivalent code with the function declared in advance.

*Example 1-3. Passing a callback as a predefined function*

```
function callback(city) {
    console.log(city);
}

cities.forEach(callback);
```

Whether your callbacks are inline functions or predefined is a matter of choice. As long as you have a reference to a function, you can use it as a callback.

# Asynchronous JavaScript

Callbacks can be invoked synchronously or asynchronously (i.e., before or after the function they are passed to returns.) The `array.forEach()` method used in the previous section invokes the callback it receives synchronously. An example of a function that invokes its callback asynchronously is `window.requestAnimationFrame()`. Its callback is invoked between browser repaint intervals, as shown in Example 1-4.

*Example 1-4. A callback being invoked asynchronously*

```
function repositionElement() {
    console.log('repositioning!');
    // ...
}

window.requestAnimationFrame(repositionElement);
console.log('I am the last line of the script');

// Console output:
// I am the last line of the script
// repositioning!
```

In this example, "I am the last line of the script" is written to the console before "repositioning!" because `requestAnimationFrame` returns immediately and invokes the `repositionElement` callback at a later time.

Synchronous code can be easier to understand because it executes in the order it is written. A good comparison can be made using the synchronous and asynchronous file APIs in Node.js. Example 1-5 is a script that writes to a file and reads back the contents synchronously. The numbered comments indicate the relative order in which some of the lines of code are executed.

*Example 1-5. Using synchronous code to write and read a file in Node.js*

```
var fs = require('fs');
var timestamp = new Date().toString();
var contents;

fs.writeFileSync('date.txt', timestamp);
contents = fs.readFileSync('date.txt');
console.log('Checking the contents');              // 1
console.assert(contents == timestamp);             // 2

console.log('I am the last line of the script'); // 3

// Console output:
// Checking the contents
// I am the last line of the script
```

The script uses the `writeFileSync` and `readFileSync` functions of the `fs` module to write a timestamp to a file and read it back. After the contents of the file are read back, they are compared to the timestamp that was originally written to see if the two values match. The `console.assert()` displays an error if the values differ. In this example they always match so the only output is from the `console.log()` statements before and after the assertion.

The script shown in Example 1-6 does the same job using the async functions `fs.writeFile()` and `fs.readFile()`. Both functions take a callback as their last parameter. The numbered comments are used again to show the relative execution order, which differs from the previous script.

*Example 1-6. Using asynchronous code to write and read a file in Node.js*

```
var fs = require('fs');
var timestamp = new Date().toString();

fs.writeFile('date.txt', timestamp, function (err) {
    if (err) throw err;

    fs.readFile('date.txt', function (err, contents) {
        if (err) throw err;
        console.log('Checking the contents');          // 2
        console.assert(contents == timestamp);          // 3
    });
});

console.log('I am the last line of the script');        // 1
```

```
// Console output:
// I am the last line of the script
// Checking the contents
```

Comparing this code to the previous example, you'll see that the console output appears in reverse order. Similar to the requestAnimationFrame example, the call to fs.writeFile() returns immediately so the last line of the script runs before the file contents are read and compared to what was written.

Although synchronous code can be easier to follow, it is also limiting. Programmers need the ability to write async code so long-running tasks such as network requests do not block other parts of the program while incomplete. Without that ability, you couldn't type in an editor at the same time your document was being autosaved or scroll through a web page while the browser was still downloading images. This is where callbacks come in. In JavaScript, callbacks are used to manage the execution order of any code that depends on an async task.

When programmers are new to asynchronous programming, it's easy for them to incorrectly expect an async script to run as if it were synchronous. Putting code that relies on the completion of an async task outside the appropriate callback creates problems. Example 1-7 shows some code that expects the callback given to readFile to be invoked before readFile returns, but when that doesn't happen the content comparison fails.

*Example 1-7. Naive asynchronous code. This doesn't work!*

```
var fs = require('fs');
var timestamp = new Date().toString();
var contents;

fs.writeFile('date.txt', timestamp);

fs.readFile('date.txt', function (err, data) {
    if (err) throw err;
    contents = data;                    // 3
});

console.log('Comparing the contents');  // 1
console.assert(timestamp == contents);  // 2 - FAIL!
```

Suppose the file only took a fraction of a millisecond to read. Does the example contain a race condition where the contents of the file are always ready for comparison when you test the code on your machine but fail every time you demo the application? The answer is that there isn't a race condition because the callback to readFile is always invoked asynchronously, so readFile is guaranteed to return before invoking the callback. Once that happens, the callback never runs before the log or assert statements on the next two lines because of the run-to-completion semantics explained in the next section. But before we get to that, a word of caution about writing functions that accept callbacks.

When you pass a callback to a function it's important to know whether the callback will be invoked synchronously or asynchronously. You don't want a series of steps that build on one another to run out of order. This is generally straightforward to determine because the function's implementation, documentation, and purpose indicate how your callback is handled. However, a function can have mixed behavior where it invokes a callback synchronously or asynchronously depending on some condition. Example 1-8 shows the jQuery.ready() function used to run code after the Document Object Model (DOM) is ready. If the DOM has finished loading before ready is invoked, the callback is invoked synchronously. Otherwise the callback is invoked once the DOM has loaded.

*Example 1-8. The jQuery.ready function can be synchronous or asynchronous*

```
jQuery.ready(function () {
    // jQuery calls this function after the DOM is loaded and ready to use
    console.log('DOM is ready');
});

console.log('I am the last line of the script');

// Console output may appear in either order depending on when the DOM is ready
```

Functions that are not consistently synchronous or asynchronous create a fork in the execution path. The jQuery.ready() function creates a fork with two paths. If a function containing the same style of mixed behavior invoked ready, there would be four possible paths. The explosion in execution branches makes explaining and testing this approach difficult, and reliable behavior in a production environment more challenging. Isaac Schlueter has written a popular blog post about this titled "Designing APIs for Asynchrony," (*http://bit.ly/apis-asynchrony*) in which he refers to the inconsistent behavior as "releasing Zalgo."

 Functions that invoke a callback synchronously in some cases and asynchronously in others create forks in the execution path that make your code less predictable.

# Run to Completion and the Event Loop

The JavaScript you write runs on a single thread, which avoids complications found in other languages that share memory between threads. But if JavaScript is single-threaded, where are the async tasks and callbacks run? To explain, let's start in Example 1-9 with a simple HTTP request in Node.

*Example 1-9. HTTP request in Node.js*

```
var http = require('http');
http.get('https://www.google.com', function (err, res) {
    console.log('got a response');
});
```

The call to `http.get()` triggers a network request that a separate thread handles. But wait—you were just told that JavaScript is single-threaded. Here's the distinction: the JavaScript code you write all runs on a single thread, but the code that implements the async tasks (the `http.get()` implementation in Example 1-9) is not part of that JavaScript and is free to run in a separate thread.

Once the task completes the result needs to be provided to the JavaScript thread. At this point the callback is placed in a queue. A multithreaded language might interrupt whatever code was currently executing to provide the results, but in JavaScript these interruptions are forbidden. Instead there is a run-to-completion rule, which means that your code runs without interruption until it passes control back to the host environment by returning from the function that the host initially called. At that point the callback can be removed from the queue and invoked.

All other threads communicate with your code by placing items on the queue. They are not permitted to manipulate any other memory accessible to JavaScript. In the previous example the callback accesses the response from the async HTTP request.

After the callback is added to the queue, there is no guarantee how long it will have to wait. How long it takes the current code to run to completion and what else is in the queue controls the time. The queue can contain things such as mouse clicks, keystrokes, and callbacks for other async tasks. The JavaScript runtime simply continues in an endless cycle of pulling an item off the queue if one is available, running the code that the item triggers, and then checking the queue again. This cycle is known as the event loop.

Figure 1-1 shows how the queue is populated and Figure 1-2 shows how the event loop processes items from the queue. All the JavaScript you write executes in the box labeled *Run JS Event Handler* in Figure 1-2. The JavaScript engine performs the rest of the activity in both diagrams behind the scenes.

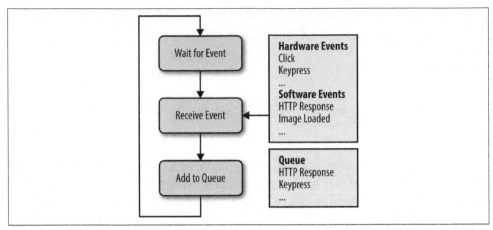

*Figure 1-1. Filling the queue*

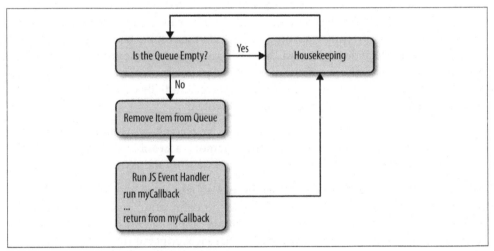

*Figure 1-2. The JavaScript event loop*

Using `setTimeout` to trigger another function after a given amount of time is a simple way to watch the event loop in action, as shown in Example 1-10. The `setTimeout` function accepts two arguments: a function to call and the minimum number of milliseconds to wait before calling the function.

*Example 1-10. Using setTimeout to demonstrate the event loop*

```
function marco() {
    console.log('polo');
}

setTimeout(marco, 0); // zero delay
```

```
console.log('Ready when you are');

// Console output:
// Ready when you are
// polo
```

The marco function is immediately placed in the queue. After the console displays "Ready when you are," the event loop turns and marco can be pulled off the queue. Notice the second parameter for setTimeout specifies the minimum amount of time that will lapse before the callback is run as opposed to the exact amount of time. It is impossible to know exactly when the callback will run because other JavaScript could be executing at that time and the machine has to let that finish before returning to the queue to invoke your callback.

Keeping in mind the run-to-completion and event loop concepts, let's revisit the XHR example given at the beginning of the chapter, which is repeated in Example 1-11 for convenience.

*Example 1-11. Async XHR (repeated from earlier)*

```
// Make an async HTTP request
var async = true;
var xhr = new XMLHttpRequest();
xhr.open('get', 'data.json', async);
xhr.send();

// Create a three second delay (don't do this in real life)
var timestamp = Date.now() + 3000;
while (Date.now() < timestamp);

// Now that three seconds have passed,
// add a listener to the xhr.load and xhr.error events
function listener() {
    console.log('greetings from listener');
}
xhr.addEventListener('load', listener);
xhr.addEventListener('error', listener);
```

The question was whether the listener function will ever be triggered. The code plays out similarly to the previous example with setTimeout. The listeners are registered after invoking the send function, but this is safe to do until the event loop turns because the runtime cannot trigger the load or error events before then.

Allowing the event loop to turn before registering the event listeners would create a race condition. Example 1-12 demonstrates that by using setTimeout.

*Example 1-12. Race condition*

```
var async = true;
var xhr = new XMLHttpRequest();
xhr.open('get', 'data.json', async);
xhr.send();

setTimeout(function delayed() { // Creates race condition!
    function listener() {
        console.log('greetings from listener');
    }
    xhr.addEventListener('load', listener);
    xhr.addEventListener('error', listener);
}, 3000);
```

Performing the event listener registration inside a callback given to `setTimeout` causes a delay. Now the only way the `listener` function will be called is if the `delayed` function is pulled off the queue and run before the HTTP request completes and the `load` or `error` event is triggered. Experimenting with different values for the delay parameter of `setTimeout` shows `listener` being invoked sometimes but not always.

## Summary

This chapter covered the underlying concepts of asynchronous JavaScript programming. Knowing how JavaScript handles callbacks allows you to control the order in which your code runs instead of writing things that work by coincidence. If the order in which your code is executed surprises you or you find yourself unsure of what will happen next, refer back to this chapter. Not only does it prepare you for using Promises, but it will make you a better JavaScript developer overall.

# CHAPTER 2

# Introducing Promises

The biggest challenge with nontrivial amounts of async JavaScript is managing execution order through a series of steps and handling any errors that arise. Promises address this problem by giving you a way to organize callbacks into discrete steps that are easier to read and maintain. And when errors occur they can be handled outside the primary application logic without the need for boilerplate checks in each step.

A promise is an object that serves as a placeholder for a value. That value is usually the result of an async operation such as an HTTP request or reading a file from disk. When an async function is called it can immediately return a promise object. Using that object, you can register callbacks that will run when the operation succeeds or an error occurs.

This chapter covers the basic ways to use promises. By the end of the chapter you should be comfortable working with functions that return promises and using promises to manage a sequence of asynchronous steps.

This book uses the Promise API for the version of JavaScript known as ECMAScript 6 (ES6.) However, there were a number of popular JavaScript Promise libraries that the development community created before ES6 that may not match the spec. These differences are mostly trivial so it is generally easy to work with different implementations once you are comfortable using standard promises. We discuss API variations and compatibility issues with other libraries in Chapter 4.

## Basic Usage

Let's walk through the basics of Promises using a series of examples beginning with a traditional callback approach and moving to an implementation using promises. Example 2-1 loads an image in a web browser and invokes a success or error callback based on the outcome.

*Example 2-1. Using callbacks*

```
loadImage('shadowfacts.png',
    function onsuccess(img) {
        // Add the image to the current web page
        document.body.appendChild(img);
    },
    function onerror(e) {
        console.log('Error occurred while loading image');
        console.log(e);
    }
);

function loadImage(url, success, error) {
    var img = new Image();
    img.src = url;

    img.onload = function () {
        success(img);
    };

    img.onerror = function (e) {
        error(e);
    };
}
```

The loadImage function uses an HTML Image object to load an image by setting the src property. The browser asynchronously loads the image based on the src and queues the onload or onerror callback after it's done.

Since loadImage is asynchronous, it accepts callbacks instead of immediately returning the image from the function. However, if loadImage was changed to return a promise you would attach the callbacks to the promise instead of passing them as arguments to the function. Example 2-2 shows how loadImage is used when it returns a promise.

*Example 2-2. Promise then and catch*

```
// Assume loadImage returns a promise
var promise = loadImage('the_general_problem.png');

promise.then(function (img) {
    document.body.appendChild(img);
});

promise.catch(function (e) {
    console.log('Error occurred while loading image');
    console.log(e);
});
```

The code indicates the following: "Load an image, then add it to the document or show an error if it can't be loaded." The promise that loadImage returns has a then method for registering a callback to use when the operation succeeds and a catch method for handling errors. However, both then and catch return promise objects so callback registration is usually done by chaining these method calls together, as shown in Example 2-3.[1]

*Example 2-3. Chaining calls using then and catch*

```
loadImage('security_holes.png').then(function (img) {
    document.body.appendChild(img);
}).catch(function (e) {
    console.log('Error occurred while loading image');
    console.log(e);
});
```

And Example 2-4 is an implementation for loadImage that returns a promise.

*Example 2-4. Creating and resolving a promise*

```
function loadImage(url) {
    var promise = new Promise(
        function resolver(resolve, reject) {
            var img = new Image();
            img.src = url;

            img.onload = function () {
                resolve(img);
            };

            img.onerror = function (e) {
                reject(e);
            };
        }
    );
    return promise;
}
```

A global constructor function called Promise exposes all the functionality for promises. In this example, loadImage creates a new promise and returns it. When Promise is used as a constructor it requires a callback known as a resolver function. The resolver serves two purposes: it receives the resolve and reject arguments, which are functions used to update the promise once the outcome is known, and any error

---

1 Chaining then and catch together also allows the catch callback to handle any errors thrown in the callback passed to then. This distinction is explained in Chapter 5.

thrown from the resolver is implicitly used to reject the promise. All the logic that was originally done in loadImage is now done inside the resolver. The resolve function is called when the image loads and reject is called if the image cannot be loaded.

When an operation represented by a promise completes, the result is stored and provided to any callbacks the promise invokes. The result is passed to the promise as a parameter of the resolve or reject functions. In the case of loadImage, the image is passed to resolve, so any callbacks registered with promise.then() will receive the image.

## Multiple Consumers

When multiple pieces of code are interested in the outcome of the same async operation, they can use the same promise. For example, you can retrieve a user's profile from the server and use it to display her name in a navigation bar. That data can also be used on an account page that displays her full profile. The code in Example 2-5 demonstrates this by using a promise to track whether a user's profile has been received. Two independent functions use the same promise to display data once it is available.

*Example 2-5. One promise with multiple consumers*

```
var user = {
    profilePromise: null,

    getProfile: function () {
        if (!this.profilePromise) {
            // Assume ajax() returns a promise that is eventually
            // fulfilled with {name: 'Samantha', subscribedToSpam: true}
            this.profilePromise = ajax(/*someurl*/);
        }
        return this.profilePromise;
    }
};

var navbar = {
    show: function (user) {
        user.getProfile().then(function (profile) {
            console.log('*** Navbar ***');
            console.log('Name: ' + profile.name);
        });
    }
};

var account = {
    show: function (user) {
        user.getProfile().then(function (profile) {
```

```
            console.log('*** Account Info ***');
            console.log('Name: ' + profile.name);
            console.log('Send lots of email? ' + profile.subscribedToSpam);
        });
    }
};

navbar.show(user);
account.show(user);

// Console output:
// *** Navbar ***
// Name: Samantha
// *** Account Info ***
// Name: Samantha
// Send lots of email? true
```

Here a user object with a `profilePromise` property and a `getProfile` method is created. The `getProfile` method returns a promise that is resolved with an object containing the user profile information. Then the script passes the user to the `navbar` and `account` objects, which display information from the profile.

Remember that a promise serves as a placeholder for the result of an operation. In this case, the `user.profilePromise` is a placeholder used by the `navbar.show()` and `account.show()` functions. These functions can be safely called anytime before or after the profile data is available. The callbacks they use to print the data to the console will only be invoked once the profile is loaded. This removes the need for an `if` statement in either function to check whether the data is ready.

In addition to that simplification, using the promise placeholder has another benefit. It removes the need for signaling inside the `getProfile` function to display the username and profile once the data is ready. The promise implicitly provides that logic, happily decoupled from the details of how or when the data is displayed.

# Promise States

The state of an operation represented by a promise is stored within the promise. At any given moment an operation has either not begun, is in progress, has run to completion, or has stopped and cannot be completed. These conditions are represented by three mutually exclusive states:

*Pending*
    The operation has not begun or is in progress.

*Fulfilled*
    The operation has completed.

*Rejected*

The operation could not be completed.

Figure 2-1 shows the relationship between the three states.

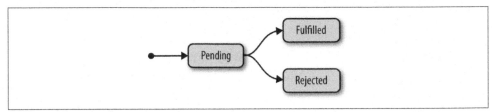

*Figure 2-1. Promise states*

In the examples so far, we refer to the fulfilled and rejected states as *success* and *error*, respectively. There is a difference between these terms. An operation could complete with an error (although that may be bad form) and an operation may not complete because it was cancelled even though no error occurred. Hence, the terms *fulfilled* and *rejected* are better descriptions for these states than *success* and *error*.

When a promise is no longer pending it is said to be *settled*. This is a general term indicating the promise has reached its final state. Once a pending promise is settled the transition is permanent. Both the state and any value given as the result cannot be changed from that point on. This behavior is consistent with how operations work in real life. A completed operation cannot become incomplete and its result does not change. Of course a program may repeat the steps of an operation multiple times. For instance, a failed operation may be retried and multiple tries may return different values. In that case, a new promise represents each try, so a more descriptive way to think of a promise is *a placeholder for the result of one attempt of an operation*.

The code in Example 2-6 demonstrates how the state of a promise can only be changed once. The code calls `resolve` and `reject` in the same promise constructor. The call to `resolve` changes the state of the promise from pending to fulfilled. Any further calls to `resolve` or `reject` are ignored because the promise is already fulfilled.

*Example 2-6. The state of a promise never changes after it is fulfilled or rejected*

```
var promise = new Promise(function (resolve, reject) {
    resolve(Math.PI);
    reject(0);                // Does nothing
    resolve(Math.sqrt(-1)); // Does nothing
});

promise.then(function (number) {
    console.log('The number is ' + number);
});
```

```
// Console output:
// The number is 3.141592653589793
```

Running the code in this example demonstrates that the calls to `reject(0)` and `resolve(Math.sqrt(-1))` have no effect because the promise has already been fulfilled with a value for Pi.

The immutability of a settled promise makes code easier to reason about. Allowing the state or value to change after a promise is fulfilled or rejected would introduce race conditions. Fortunately, the state transition rules for promises prevent that problem.

Since the `reject` function transitions a promise to the rejected state, why does the `resolve` function transition a promise to a state called *fulfilled* instead of *resolved*? Resolving a promise is not the same as fulfilling it. When the argument passed to `resolve` is a value, the promise is immediately fulfilled. However, when another promise is passed to `resolve`, such as `promise.resolve(otherPromise)`, the promises are bound together. If the promise passed to `resolve` is fulfilled, then both promises will be fulfilled. And if the promise passed to `resolve` is rejected, then both promises will be rejected. In short, the argument passed to `resolve` dictates the fate of the promise. Figure 2-2 shows this process.

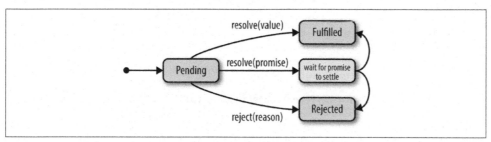

*Figure 2-2. Resolving or rejecting a promise*

The `resolve` and `reject` functions can be called without an argument, in which case the fulfillment value or rejection reason will be the JavaScript type `undefined`.

The Promise API also provides two convenience methods (see Example 2-7) for creating a promise that is immediately resolved or rejected: `Promise.resolve()` and `Promise.reject()`.

*Example 2-7. Convenience functions for resolve and reject*

```
// Equivalent ways to create a resolved promise
new Promise(function (resolve, reject) {
    resolve('the long way')
});
Promise.resolve('the short way');
```

```
// Equivalent ways to create a rejected promise
new Promise(function (resolve, reject) {
    reject('long rejection')
});
Promise.reject('short rejection');
```

These convenience functions are useful when you already have the item that should be used to resolve or reject the promise. Some of the code samples that follow use these functions instead of the traditional Promise constructor to concisely create a promise with the desired state.

# Chaining Promises

We've seen how then and catch return promises for easy method chaining, however they do not return a reference to the same promise. Every time either of these methods is called a new promise is created and returned. Example 2-8 is an explicit example of then returning a new promise.

*Example 2-8. Calls to then always return a new promise*

```
var p1, p2;

p1 = Promise.resolve();
p2 = p1.then(function () {
    // ...
});

console.log('p1 and p2 are different objects: ' + (p1 !== p2));

// Console output:
// p1 and p2 are different objects: true
```

Example 2-9 shows how new promises returned by then can be chained together to execute a sequence of steps.

*Example 2-9. Using then to sequence multiple steps*

```
step1().then(
    function step2(resultFromStep1) {
        // ...
    }
).then(
    function step3(resultFromStep2) {
        // ...
    }
).then(
    function step4(resultFromStep3) {
```

```
        // ...
    }
);
```

Each call to then returns a new promise you can use to attach another callback. Whatever value is returned from that callback resolves the new promise. This pattern allows each step to send its return value to the next step. If a step returns a promise instead of a value, the following step receives whatever value is used to fulfill that promise. Example 2-10 shows all the ways to fulfill a promise created by then.

*Example 2-10. Passing values in a sequence of steps*

```
Promise.resolve('ta-da!').then(
    function step2(result) {
        console.log('Step 2 received ' + result);
        return 'Greetings from step 2';        // Explicit return value
    }
).then(
    function step3(result) {
        console.log('Step 3 received ' + result);    // No explicit return value
    }
).then(
    function step4(result) {
        console.log('Step 4 received ' + result);
        return Promise.resolve('fulfilled value');    // Return a promise
    }
).then(
    function step5(result) {
        console.log('Step 5 received ' + result);
    }
);

// Console output:
// Step 2 received ta-da!
// Step 3 received Greetings from step 2
// Step 4 received undefined
// Step 5 received fulfilled value
```

An explicitly returned value resolves the promise that wraps step2. Since step3 does not explicitly return a value, undefined fulfills that promise. And the value from the promise explicitly returned in step4 fulfills the promise that wraps step4.

# Callback Execution Order

Promises are primarily used to manage the order in which code is run relative to other tasks. The previous chapter demonstrated how problems occur when async callbacks are expected to run synchronously. You can avoid these problems by understanding which callbacks in the Promise API are synchronous and which are asynchronous. Fortunately there are only two cases. The resolver function passed to the Promise constructor executes synchronously. And all callbacks passed to then and catch are invoked asynchronously. Example 2-11 shows a Promise constructor and an onFulfilled callback with some logging statements to demonstrate the order. The numbered comments show the relative execution order.

*Example 2-11. Execution order of callbacks used by promises*

```
var promise = new Promise(function (resolve, reject) {
    console.log('Inside the resolver function');       // 1
    resolve();
});

promise.then(function () {
   console.log('Inside the onFulfilled handler');       // 3
});

console.log('This is the last line of the script');     // 2

// Console output:
// Inside the resolver function
// This is the last line of the script
// Inside the onFulfilled handler
```

This example is similar to the synchronous and asynchronous callback code in the previous chapter. You can see that the resolver function passed to the Promise constructor executes immediately followed by the log statement at the end of the script. Then the event loop turns and the promise that is already resolved invokes the onFulfilled handler. Although the example code is trivial, understanding the execution order is a key part of using promises effectively. If you do not feel confident predicting the execution order of any of the examples so far, consider reviewing the material in Chapter 1 and this section.

## Basic Error Propagation

Error propagation and handling is a significant aspect of working with promises. This section introduces the basic concepts while all of Chapter 5 is dedicated to this topic.

Rejections and errors propagate through promise chains. When one promise is rejected all subsequent promises in the chain are rejected in a domino effect until an onRejected handler is found. In practice, one catch function is used at the end of a chain (see Example 2-12) to handle all rejections. This approach treats the chain as a single unit that the fulfilled or rejected final promise represents.

*Example 2-12. Using a rejection handler at the end of a chain*

```
Promise.reject(Error('bad news')).then(
    function step2() {
        console.log('This is never run');
    }
).then(
    function step3() {
        console.log('This is also never run');
    }
).catch(
    function (error) {
        console.log('Something failed along the way. Inspect error for more info.');
        console.log(error); // Error object with message: 'bad news'
    }
);

// Console output:
// Something failed along the way. Inspect error for more info.
// [Error object] { message: 'bad news' ... }
```

This code begins a chain of promises by creating a rejected promise using `Promise.reject()`. Two more promises follow that are created by adding calls to then and finished with a call to `catch` to handle rejections.

Notice the code in `step2` and `step3` never runs. These functions are only called when the promise they are attached to is fulfilled. Since the promise at the top of the chain was rejected, all subsequent callbacks in the chain are ignored until the `catch` handler is reached.

Promises are also rejected when an error is thrown in a callback passed to then or in the resolver function passed to the Promise constructor. Example 2-13 is similar to the last, except throwing an error instead of using the `Promise.reject()` function now rejects the promise.

*Example 2-13. Rejecting a promise by throwing an error in the constructor callback*

```
rejectWith('bad news').then(
    function step2() {
        console.log('This is never run');
    }
).catch(
    function (error) {
        console.log('Foiled again!');
        console.log(error); // Error object with message: 'bad news'
    }
);

function rejectWith(val) {
    return new Promise(function (resolve, reject) {
```

```
        throw Error(val);
        resolve('Not used'); // This line is never run
    });
}

// Console output:
// Foiled again!
// [Error object] { message: 'bad news' ... }
```

Both examples in this section provided a JavaScript Error object when rejecting the promise. Although any value, including undefined, can reject promises, we recommend using an error object. Creating an error can capture the call stack for troubleshooting and makes it easier to treat the argument the catch handler receives in a uniform way.

 Using JavaScript Error objects to reject promises can capture the call stack for troubleshooting and makes it easier to treat the argument the catch handler receives in a uniform way.

# The Promise API

The complete Promise API consists of a constructor and six functions, four of which have already been demonstrated. However, it's worth describing each of them so you can see the API as a whole and be aware of optional arguments.

**Promise**

```
new Promise(function (resolve, reject) { … }) returns promise
```

The Promise global is a constructor function that the new keyword invokes.

The Promise global creates promise objects that have the two methods then and catch for registering callbacks that are invoked once the promise is fulfilled or rejected.

**promise.then**

```
promise.then([onFulfilled], [onRejected]) returns promise
```

The promise.then() method accepts an onFulfilled callback and an onRejected callback. People generally register onRejected callbacks using promise.catch() instead of passing a second argument to then (see the explanation provided in Chapter 5.) The function then returns a promise that is resolved by the return value of the onFulfilled or onRejected callback. Any error thrown inside the callback rejects the new promise with that error.

## promise.catch

```
promise.catch(onRejected) returns promise
```

The `promise.catch()` method accepts an `onRejected` callback and returns a promise that the return value of the callback or any error thrown by the callback resolves or rejects, respectively. That means any rejection the callback given to `catch` handles is not propagated further unless you explicitly use `throw` inside the callback.

## Promise.resolve

```
Promise.resolve([value|promise]) returns promise
```

The `Promise.resolve()` function is a convenience function for creating a promise that is already resolved with a given value. If you pass a promise as the argument to `Promise.resolve()`, the new promise is bound to the promise you provided and it will be fulfilled or rejected accordingly.

## Promise.reject

```
Promise.reject([reason]) returns promise
```

The `Promise.reject()` function is a convenience function for creating a rejected promise with a given reason.

## Promise.all

```
Promise.all(iterable) returns promise
```

The `Promise.all()` function maps a series of promises to their fulfillment values. It accepts an iterable object such as an `Array`, a `Set`, or a custom iterable. The function returns a new promise fulfilled by an array containing the values in the iterable. Corresponding fulfillment values in the resulting array replace any promises contained in the iterable. The new promise that the function returns is only fulfilled after all the promises in the iterable are fulfilled, or it is rejected as soon as any of the promises in the iterable are rejected. If the new promise is rejected it contains the rejection reason from the promise in the iterable that triggered the rejection. If you are working with a Promise implementation that does not understand ES6 iterables, it will likely expect standard arrays instead.

---

### What Is an Iterable?

An iterable is an object that provides a series of values by implementing a predefined interface (also known as a protocol.) Iterables are specified in ES6 and explained in "Iterables and Iterators" on page 68.

---

**`Promise.race`**

```
Promise.race(iterable) returns promise
```

The `Promise.race()` function reduces a series of items to the first available value. It accepts an iterable and returns a new promise. The function examines each item in the iterable until it finds either an item that is not a promise or a promise that has been settled. The returned promise is then fulfilled or rejected based on that item. If the iterable only contains unsettled promises, the returned promise is settled once one of the promises in the iterable is settled.

# Summary

This chapter introduced all the basic concepts of Promises. Keep these three points in mind:

- A promise is a placeholder for a value that is usually the result of an asynchronous operation.
- A promise has three states: pending, fulfilled, and rejected.
- After a promise is fulfilled or rejected, its state and value can never be changed.

At this point you have walked through a number of examples that demonstrate the basic ways a promise is used and you are ready to run sequential asynchronous steps in your own code using promise chains. You should also be comfortable using APIs that return promises for asynchronous work.

One example of promises in the wild is in the CSS Font Load Events spec, which provides a `FontFaceSet.load()` function that returns a promise for loading fonts into the browser. Consider how you could use this function to only display text once a desired font is loaded in the browser.

Promises can be combined to orchestrate async tasks and structure code in various ways. Although a sequential workflow was provided here, you'll soon want to use promises in more advanced ways. The next chapter walks through a variety of ways you can use promises in your applications.

# CHAPTER 3

# Working with Standard Promises

We've covered the standard Promise API and some basic scenarios, but like any technology, that's only part of the story. Now it's time for scenarios you'll encounter and techniques you can use while writing real-world applications.

## The Async Ripple Effect

Async functions and promises are contagious. After you start using them they naturally spread through your code. When you have one async function, any code that calls that function now contains an async step. The process of other functions becoming async by extension creates a ripple effect that continues all the way through the call stack. This is shown in Example 3-1 using three functions. Look how the async ajax function forces the other functions to also be async.

*Example 3-1. The async ripple effect*

```
showPun().then(function () {
    console.log('Maybe I should stick to programming');
});

function showPun() {
    return getPun().then(function (pun) {
        console.log(pun);
    });
}

function getPun() {
    // Assume ajax() returns a promise that is eventually
    // fulfilled by json for {content: 'The pet store job was ruff!'}
    return ajax(/*someurl*/).then(function (json) {
        var pun = JSON.parse(json);
```

```
        return pun.content;
    });
}

// Console output:
// The pet store job was ruff!
// Maybe I should stick to programming
```

The work to retrieve and display a pun is divided into three functions: showPun, getPun, and ajax. The functions form a chain of promises that starts with ajax and ends with the object returned by showPun. The ajax function returns a promise representing the result of an async XHR request. If ajax returned the JSON synchronously, getPun and showPun would not consume or return promises.

As a general rule, any function that uses a promise should also return a promise. When a promise is not propagated, the calling code cannot know when the promise is fulfilled and thus cannot effectively perform work after the fact. It's easy to ignore this rule when writing a function whose caller does not care when the async work is finished, but don't be fooled. It's much easier to return a promise that initially goes unused than to retrofit promises into a series of functions later on.

## Conditional Logic

It's common to have a workflow that contains a conditional step. For instance, some actions may require user authentication. However, once a user is authenticated, he does not need to repeat that step every time the action is taken.

As an example, we'll use an electronic book reader that requires authentication before the user can access any other features. There are multiple ways to code this scenario. Example 3-2 shows a first pass.

*Example 3-2. Conditional async step*

```
var user = {
    authenticated: false,

    login: function () {
        // Returns a promise for the login request
        // Set authenticated to true and fulfill promise when login succeeds
    }
};

// Avoid this style of conditional async execution
function showMainMenu() {
    if (!user.authenticated) {
        user.login().then(showMainMenu);
        return;
    }
```

```
    // ... Code to display main menu
};
```

In this implementation of showMainMenu, the menu is displayed immediately if the user is already authenticated. If the user is not authenticated, the async login process is performed and showMenu is run again once the login succeeds.

One problem here is that the menu will silently fail to display if the login process fails. That's because showMainMenu relies on a promise but does not return a promise as described in the preceding section.

A second problem is that showMainMenu may behave synchronously or asynchronously depending on whether the user is already authenticated. As described in Chapter 1, this style of code creates multiple execution paths that can be difficult to reason about and create inconsistent behavior.

As shown in Example 3-3, the issues in showMainMenu can be addressed by substituting a resolved promise if the user is already authenticated.

*Example 3-3. Substituting a resolved promise*

```
function showMainMenu() {
    var p = (!user.authenticated) ? user.login() : Promise.resolve();
    return p.then(function () {
        // ... Code to display main menu
    });
}
```

Now the menu is always displayed asynchronously using either the promise that user.login() returned or a resolved promise substituted for the login process.

You can eliminate the need for a substitute promise by calling user.login() every time, as shown in Example 3-4.

*Example 3-4. Encapsulating conditional logic with a promise*

```
function showMainMenu() {
    return user.login().then(function () {
        // ... Code to display main menu
    });
}
```

This doesn't mean all the login steps need to be repeated every time. The promise that login returned can be cached and reused, as shown in Example 3-5.

*Example 3-5. Caching a promise*

```
var user = {
    loginPromise: null,

    login: function () {
        var me = this;
        if (this.loginPromise == null) {
            this.loginPromise = ajax(/*someurl*/);

            // Remove cached loginPromise when a failure occurs to allow retry
            this.loginPromise.catch(function () {
                me.loginPromise = null;
            });
        }
        return this.loginPromise;
    }
};
```

In Example 3-5, the `loginPromise` is created the first time `login` is called. All subsequent calls to login return the same promise as long as the login process does not fail. In case of failure, the cached promise is removed so the process can be retried.

# Parallel Execution

Multiple asynchronous tasks can be run in parallel, as shown in Example 3-6. Consider a financial website that shows an updated balance for all your bank accounts and credit cards each time you log in. The updated balance from each institution can be requested in parallel and displayed as soon as it is received.

*Example 3-6. Running asynchronous tasks in parallel*

```
// Define each account
var accounts = ['Checking Account', 'Travel Rewards Card', 'Big Box Retail Card'];

console.log('Updating balance information...');
accounts.forEach(function (account) {
    // ajax() returns a promise eventually fulfilled by the account balance
    ajax(/*someurl for account*/).then(function (balance) {
        console.log(account + ' Balance: ' + balance);
    });
});

// Console output:
// Updating balance information...
// Checking Account Balance: 384
// Travel Rewards Card Balance: 509
// Big Box Retail Card Balance: 0
```

Promises are also good for consolidating parallel tasks into a single outcome. Suppose a message should be displayed informing the user when all the account balances are up-to-date. You can create a consolidated promise using the `Promise.all()` function that maps promises to their outcomes, as explained in Example 3-7. A full description of this function is provided in "The Promise API" on page 22. In short, `Promise.all()` returns a new promise that is fulfilled when all the promises it receives are fulfilled. And if any of the promises it receives get rejected, the new promise is also rejected.

*Example 3-7. Consolidating the outcomes of parallel tasks with Promise.all()*

```
var requests = accounts.map(function (account) {
    return ajax(/*someurl for account*/);
});

// Update status message once all requests are fulfilled
Promise.all(requests).then(function (balances) {
    console.log('All ' + balances.length + ' balances are up to date');
}).catch(function (error) {
    console.log('An error occurred while retrieving balance information');
    console.log(error);
});

// Console output:
// All 3 balances are up to date
```

Instead of looping through the accounts using `forEach`, the `map` function is used to create an array of promises representing a balance request for each account. `Promise.all()` then consolidates the promises into a single promise. An array containing all the account balances resolves the consolidated promise. In this example the `length` property of that array is used to display the number of balances retrieved.

You can also wait for all the operations represented by some promises to settle regardless of whether they succeeded or failed. In Example 3-8, let's revise Example 3-7 to show the number of balances that were updated even if some requests failed.

*Example 3-8. Running code after multiple operations have finished, regardless of their outcome*

```
function settled(promises) {
    var alwaysFulfilled = promises.map(function (p) {
        return p.then(
            function onFulfilled(value) {
                return { state: 'fulfilled', value: value };
            },
            function onRejected(reason) {
```

```
                return { state: 'rejected', reason: reason };
            }
        );
    });
    return Promise.all(alwaysFulfilled);
}

// Update status message once all requests finish
settled(requests).then(function (outcomes) {
    var count = 0;
outcomes.forEach(function (outcome) {
    if (outcome.state == 'fulfilled') count++;
});
    console.log(count + ' out of ' + outcomes.length + ' balances were updated');
});

// Console output (varies based on requests):
// 2 balances out of 3 were updated
```

The settled function consolidates an array of promises into a single promise that is fulfilled once all the promises in the array are settled. An array of objects that indicate the outcome of each promise fulfills the new promise. In this example, the array of outcomes is reduced[1] to a single value representing the number of requests that succeeded.[2]

## Sequential Execution Using Loops or Recursion

You can dynamically build a chain of promises to run tasks in sequential order (i.e., each task must wait for the preceding task to finish before it begins.) Most of the examples so far have demonstrated sequential chains of then calls built with a predefined number of steps. But it is common to have an array where each item requires its own async task, like the code in Example 3-6 that looped through an array of accounts to get the balance for each one. Those balances were retrieved in parallel but there are times when you want to run tasks serially. For instance, if each task requires significant bandwidth or computation, you may want to throttle the amount of work being done.

Before building a sequential chain, let's start with code that runs a set of tasks in parallel, as shown in Example 3-9, based on the items in an array similar to Example 3-6.

---

1 It is natural to use outcomes.reduce() in place of outcomes.forEach() in this example; however, some readers may be unfamiliar with reduce, so it is not used until it is explained in the next section (see Example 3-10).

2 The settled function is based on a similar function in the Bluebird library.

---

*Example 3-9. Running tasks in parallel using a loop*

```
var products = ['sku-1', 'sku-2', 'sku-3'];

products.forEach(function (sku) {
    getInfo(sku).then(function (info) {
        console.log(info)
    });
});

function getInfo(sku) {
    console.log('Requested info for ' + sku);
    return ajax(/*someurl for sku*/);
}

// Console output:
// Requested info for sku-1
// Requested info for sku-2
// Requested info for sku-3
// Info for sku-1
// Info for sku-2
// Info for sku-3
```

This code iterates through an array of products and calls the getInfo function for each one. The beginning of each request is logged to the console inside getInfo and the outcome of each request is logged inside the loop after completing the request. You can see the requests are run in parallel because the code inside the forEach does not use any promises that previous iterations of the loop created. The order of the console output also demonstrates the parallel nature of the code. All three requests are made before the first result is received.

Let's move from parallel tasks to sequential chains. The code we'll use to do that can be daunting if you are unfamiliar with the array reduce function, which distills the elements of an array to a single value. Example 3-10 provides a snippet to serve as an introduction/refresher on how reduce is used.

*Example 3-10. Overview of array.reduce*

```
finalResult = array.reduce(function (previousValue, currentValue) {
    // Create a result using the previousValue and currentValue
    // return the result which will be used as the previousValue in the next loop
    return previousValue + currentValue;
}, initialValue) // Used with first element
```

The reduce function accepts a callback that is invoked for each element in the array. It receives the previous value returned from the callback and the current element in the array. The previous value in the callback is seeded with an initial value the first time the callback is invoked. The return value for reduce is whatever the callback returns when it is invoked for the last element in the array.

Example 3-11 uses reduce to calculate the sum of all the numbers in an array.

*Example 3-11. Simple array.reduce to sum numbers*

```
var numbers = [2, 4, 6];
var sum = numbers.reduce(function (sum, number) {
    return sum + number;
}, 0);
console.log(sum);

// Console output:
// 12
```

You could write some code with a for loop that would accomplish the same thing as reduce but it would be clunky by comparison. Now let's get back to running tasks sequentially using reduce.

Example 3-12 uses the same products array and getInfo function from earlier code to request and display information. However, no request is started until the previous one completes. Although this could be done by calling the reduce function on products directly, the logic has been abstracted into a function called sequence.

*Example 3-12. Build a sequential chain using a loop*

```
// Build a sequential chain of promises from the elements in an array
function sequence(array, callback) {
    return array.reduce(function chain(promise, item) {
        return promise.then(function () {
            return callback(item);
        });
    }, Promise.resolve());
};

var products = ['sku-1', 'sku-2', 'sku-3'];

sequence(products, function (sku) {
    return getInfo(sku).then(function (info) {
        console.log(info)
    });
}).catch(function (reason) {
    console.log(reason);
});

function getInfo(sku) {
    console.log('Requested info for ' + sku);
    return ajax(/*someurl for sku*/);
```

```
}
```

```
// Console output:
// Requested info for sku-1
// Info for sku-1
// Requested info for sku-2
// Info for sku-2
// Requested info for sku-3
// Info for sku-3
```

Skip the implementation of sequence for a moment and look at how it is used. An array of products is passed in along with a callback that is invoked once for each product in the array. If the callback returns a promise, the next callback is not invoked until that promise is fulfilled. The console output shows that the requests are run sequentially.

The sequence function encapsulates the details of chaining promises to dynamically sequence tasks. It iterates over the array by calling reduce and seeding the previous value with a resolved promise. The chain function given to reduce always returns a promise that the return value of the callback passed into sequence resolves. The cycle continues for each element until exhausting the array and returning the last promise in the chain. The calling code attaches a catch handler to that promise to conveniently handle any problems.

You can also construct a sequence of tasks from a list using recursion by replacing the previous sequence implementation in Example 3-12 with the code in Example 3-13.

*Example 3-13. Build sequential chain using recursion*

```
// Replaces sequence in previous example with a recursive implementation
function sequence(array, callback) {
    function chain(array, index) {
        if (index == array.length) return Promise.resolve();
        return Promise.resolve(callback(array[index])).then(function () {
            return chain(array, index + 1);
        });
    }
    return chain(array, 0);
};
```

```
// Console output is identical to the previous example
```

Here the reduce function from earlier is replaced by chain, which recursively calls itself for each element in the array. A risk in recursive programming is creating a stack overflow by making too many recursive calls in a row. Fortunately, that does not occur here because a separate turn of the event loop invokes the promise callbacks, so each recursive call to chain is at the top of the call stack.

Although using recursion in Example 3-12 has the same final outcome as building the chain with a loop, there is an interesting difference between the two approaches. Using a loop builds the entire chain of promises at the outset without waiting for any of the promises to be resolved. The recursive approach adds to the chain on demand after resolving the preceding promise. A major benefit of the on-demand approach is the ability to decide whether to continue chaining promises based on the result from the preceding promise.

The last few examples have made a chain with a predefined number of steps based on the elements in an array. With recursion you can build a chain whose length is not determined in advance, as shown in Example 3-14. A great example for this case is included in the WHATWG Streams specification (*http://bit.ly/whatwg_streams*) for performing I/O. The spec contains sample code for sequentially reading all the data from a stream in a series of chunks. Each call to read returns a promise fulfilled by an object with a value property containing a chunk of data and a done property indicating when the stream is exhausted.[3]

*Example 3-14. Conditionally expanding a chain based on the outcome of a preceding promise*

```
function readAllChunks(readableStream) {
    var reader = readableStream.getReader();
    var chunks = [];

    return pump();

    function pump() {
        return reader.read().then(function (result) {
            if (result.done) {
                return chunks;
            }

            chunks.push(result.value);
            return pump();
        });
    };
}
```

Here the pump function appends each chunk of data to an array and recursively calls itself until result.done signals there is no more data available.

---

3 The code in the spec uses object destructuring with an arrow function, which has been replaced by a traditional function declaration here. Destructuring and arrow functions are discussed in Chapter 6.

You may not have an immediate need for building sequential promise chains, but it will inevitably occur. If you use a library to supplement standard promises, this functionality may be included. Libraries are discussed in more detail in Chapter 4.

 Building long chains of promises may require significant amounts of memory. Be sure to instrument and test your code to guard against unexpected performance problems.

# Managing Latency

When you have a promise that wraps an asynchronous network request, how long should you wait for the promise to settle? Although you may expect a quick response, the actual time is based on many factors outside the control of your code. You can prevent your application from entering a state of prolonged or endless waiting by enforcing a time limit.

The getData function in Example 3-15 returns a promise fulfilled by fresh data fetched from a server. It concurrently pulls existing data from a cache to use in case the server does not respond quickly enough. And if neither the server nor the cache respond in time, the promise returned by getData is rejected. Each of the outcomes is represented by a promise. The code uses Promise.race() to select the first available outcome.

*Example 3-15. Manage response time using Promise.race()*

```
function getData() {
    var timeAllowed = 500; // milliseconds
    var deadline = Date.now() + timeAllowed;

    var freshData = ajax(/*someurl*/);

    var cachedData = fetchFromCache().then(function (data) {
        return new Promise(function (resolve) {
            var timeRemaining = Math.max(deadline - Date.now(), 0);
            setTimeout(function () {
                resolve(data);
            }, timeRemaining);
        });
    });

    var failure = new Promise(function (resolve, reject) {
        setTimeout(function () {
            reject(new Error('Unable to fetch data in allotted time'));
        }, timeAllowed);
    });
```

```
    return Promise.race([freshData, cachedData, failure]);
}
```

Some scenarios were omitted from the preceding example so that they would not detract from the point. For instance, if the network request fails quickly, the promise returned from `getData` will be rejected immediately. In this case you may still want to use the cached data if it is retrieved within the allotted time. Reactive programming libraries such as RxJS, Bacon.js, and Kefir.js are specifically intended for scenarios like this.

# Functional Composition

Earlier in the book you saw how promise chains are useful in orchestrating a series of async steps. The same pattern is also good for building pipelines of functions. This technique of combining several basic functions into a more powerful composite is known as *functional composition*, and it divides code into discrete units that are easier to test and maintain.

Let's use a website for a large real estate agency in Example 3-16. Each agent in the company has a web page with her picture and contact information. All the profile photos are displayed in the same size in black and white and include the company name. You can create a pipeline that processes images for display on the site.

*Example 3-16. Verbose pipeline*

```
// Generic image processing functions
function scaleToFit(width, height, image) {
    console.log('Scaling image to ' + width + ' x ' + height);
    return image;
}

function watermark(text, image) {
    console.log('Watermarking image with ' + text);
    return image;
}

function grayscale(image) {
    console.log('Converting image to grayscale');
    return image;
}

// Image processing pipeline
function processImage(image) {
    return scaleToFit(300, 450, image).then(function (image) {
        return watermark('The Real Estate Company', image);
    }).then(function (image) {
        return grayscale(image);
```

```
        });
}

// Console output for processImage():
// Scaling image to 300 x 450
// Watermarking image with The Real Estate Company
// Converting image to grayscale
```

The image processing functions in this example are all generic. They have no knowledge of the real estate website and could easily exist in a third-party library. The `processImage` function containing the pipeline is the only thing with domain-specific knowledge. It composes the three functions in the required order and provides the necessary parameters.

The `processImage` function can be shortened, as shown in Example 3-17, by replacing the traditional-looking promise chain with a chain of functions preconfigured with the necessary parameters for width, height, and watermark text.

*Example 3-17. Concise pipeline*

```
// Replaces processImage in previous example
function processImage(image) {
    // Image is always last parameter preceded by any configuration parameters
    var customScaleToFit = scaleToFit.bind(null, 300, 450);
    var customWatermark = watermark.bind(null, 'The Real Estate Company');

    return Promise.resolve(image)
        .then(customScaleToFit)
        .then(customWatermark)
        .then(grayscale);
}
```

The pipeline is succinctly written at the end of `processImage`. The code works because each of the functions that manipulate the image take it as the last parameter, allowing the width, height, and watermark parameters to be bound in advance.

Using promise chains in this manner does not require the individual functions to be async. However, it does allow any of the functions in the chain to change from synchronous to asynchronous later without affecting the calling code. Just avoid overkill with this approach by using it whenever you can, as opposed to only when you should. For example, you may not need a chain of promises when a call to the built-in `map` or `filter` array functions will do.

# Summary

This chapter covered a number of scenarios that are likely to arise when using promises. It showed how one async function affects all the functions that come before it in the call stack. It also showed how to process an arbitrary number of tasks sequentially or in parallel. And how to build processing pipelines by chaining promises together.

All the topics in this chapter were addressed using the standard Promise API. This discussion is continued in Chapter 4 using expanded APIs that some promise libraries and frameworks provided.

# Using Libraries and Frameworks

Before the ES6 Promise API existed, many JavaScript libraries and frameworks implemented their own version of Promises. Some libraries were written for the sole purpose of providing promises while established libraries like jQuery added them to handle their async APIs.

Promise libraries can act as polyfills in older web browsers and other environments where native promises are not provided. They can also supplement the standard API with a wide set of functions for managing promises. If your code only uses promises that you create you're in a good position to choose a library and take full advantage of its extended API. And if you are handling promises that other libraries produced, you can wrap those promises with ones from your chosen library to access the additional features.

This chapter focuses on nonnative promise implementations. The majority of the chapter covers Bluebird, a fast and robust promise library. Although Bluebird is a compelling choice, there are other good options. For example, the Q promise library predates Bluebird and is widely used in applications and frameworks including AngularJS. Q and other libraries are not discussed in detail because this chapter is not a guide to choosing between libraries. It is an introduction to the enhancements that third-party libraries offer to demonstrate their value. The Promise implementation in jQuery is also discussed because of jQuery's immense popularity. However, this is not a complete walk-through of either Bluebird or jQuery. These open source projects evolve rapidly, so refer to the official online documentation for full details of the current features.

# Promise Interoperability and Thenables

Before diving into the details of specific libraries, let's discuss how promises from different libraries can be used with one another. The basis of all interoperability between promise implementations is the *thenable* contract. Any object with a then(onFulfilled, onRejected) method can be wrapped by any standard promise implementation.

As Kris Kowal wrote when reviewing this chapter, "...regardless of what that method returns, regardless of what onFulfilled and onRejected return, and in fact regardless of whether onFulfilled or onRejected are executed synchronously or asynchronously, [then] is sufficient for any of these Promise implementations to coerce the thenable into a well-behaved, always-asynchronous, always returning capital-P Promise, promise. This is particularly important when consuming promises from unreliable third parties, where unreliable can be as innocuous as a backward-incompatible version of the same library."

Example 4-1 shows an example of a simple thenable object wrapped with a standard promise.

*Example 4-1. Wrapping a thenable for interoperability*

```
function thenable(value) {
    return {
        then: function (onfulfill, onreject) {
            onfulfill(value);
        }
    };
}

var promise = Promise.resolve(thenable('voila!'));
promise.then(function(result) {
    console.log(result);
});

// Console output:
// voila!
```

Although it is unlikely you will encounter such a sparse thenable in your own code, the same concept applies to wrapping promises from other implementations to work as the promise implementation that your code prefers.

# The Bluebird Promise Library

Bluebird is an open source promise library with a rich API and excellent performance. The Bluebird GitHub repo includes benchmarks that show it outperforming other implementations, including the native version in the V8 JavaScript engine used by Node.js and Google Chrome. Bluebird's author Petka Antonov says native implementations are more focused on matching behavior specifications than performance optimization, which allows carefully tuned JavaScript to outperform native code.

Bluebird offers many other features including elegant ways of managing execution context, wrapping Node.js APIs, working with collections of promises, and manipulating fulfillment values.

## Loading Bluebird

When Bluebird is included in a web page using a `script` tag, it overwrites the global Promise object by default with its own version of Promise. Bluebird can also be loaded in the browser in other ways, such as an AMD module using require.js, and it is available as an npm package for use in Node.js.

The Bluebird Promise object can serve as a drop-in replacement or polyfill for the ES6 Promise. When the Bluebird script is loaded in a web browser it overwrites the global Promise object. However, you can use `Promise.noConflict()` after loading Bluebird to restore the global Promise object to its previous reference in order to run Bluebird side by side with native promises. As explained in the earlier section on interoperability and thenables, you can treat other promise implementations as Bluebird promises by wrapping them using `[Bluebird Promise].resolve(promise)`. In Example 4-2, Bluebird wraps a native promise to expose functions that reveal its state.

*Example 4-2. Wrap a native promise with a Bluebird promise*

```
// Assume bluebird has been loaded using <script src="bluebird.js"></script>
var Bluebird = Promise.noConflict();  // Restore previous reference to Promise
var nativePromise = Promise.resolve(); // Native Promise
var b = Bluebird.resolve(nativePromise); // Wrap native promise with Bluebird promise

console.log('Pending? ' + b.isPending());     // Pending? false
console.log('Fulfilled? ' + b.isFulfilled()); // Fulfilled? true
console.log('Rejected? ' + b.isRejected());   // Rejected? false
```

The remaining examples in this chapter that relate to Bluebird assume that all promises are Bluebird promises.

## Managing Execution Context

Callbacks frequently need access to variables in their enclosing scope. Two common ways of accessing those variables are shown in the `configure` and `print` methods in Example 4-3. Both access the `pageSize` property of a printer object.

*Example 4-3. Using the enclosing scope through function.bind() or aliasing*

```
var printer = {
    pageSize: 'US LETTER',

    connect: function () {
        // Return a promise that is fulfilled when a connection
        // to the printer is established
    },

    configure: function (pageSize) {
        return this.connect().then(function () {
            console.log('Setting page size to ' + pageSize);
            this.pageSize = pageSize;
        }.bind(this)); // Using bind to set the context
    },

    print: function (job) {
        // Aliasing the outer context
        // _this, that, and self are some other common alias names
        var me = this;

        return this.connect().then(function () {
            console.log('Printing job using page size ' + me.pageSize);
        });
    }
};

printer.configure('A4').then(function () {
    return printer.print('Test page');
});

// Console output:
// Setting page size to A4
// Printing job using page size A4
```

The `configure` method uses `bind(this)` to share its context with the inner callback. The `print` method aliases the outer context to a variable called `me` in order to access it inside the callback.

Bluebird offers an alternative way of exposing the enclosing scope by adding a `promise.bind()` method that sets the context for all subsequent callbacks used in a promise chain, as shown in Example 4-4.

*Example 4-4. Setting callback contexts using promise.bind()*

```
printer.shutdown = function () {
    this.connect().bind(this).then(function() {  // bluebird.bind not function.bind
        console.log('First callback can use ' + this.paperSize);
    }).then(function () {
        console.log('And second callback can use ' + this.paperSize);
```

```
    });
};
```

```
// Console.output:
// First callback can use A4
// And second callback can use A4
```

Using `bluebirdPromise.bind()` has an advantage over the previous two solutions because it removes the call to `bind` for individual functions in a long chain and avoids adding a reference to the enclosing scope of each callback.

The effect of `bind` applies to all subsequently chained promises, even those on a promise that a function returns. To avoid leaking objects used as the context in `bind`, you can mask the effect by calling `bind` again before returning a bound promise chain from a function. This practice is even more important if the function is being consumed as a third-party library.

Example 4-5 shows an updated version of the `printer.shutdown()` method that masks the printer context that the callbacks inside it use.

*Example 4-5. Hiding the bound context from calling code*

```
printer.shutdown = function () {
    return this.connect().bind(this).then(function () {
        //...
    }).then(function () {
        //...
    }).bind(); // mask the previous binding
};
```

```
printer.shutdown().then(function () {
    console.log('Not running in the context of the printer: ' + this !== printer);
});
```

```
// Console.output:
// This code is not running in the context of the printer: true
```

# Wrapping Node.js Functions

Node.js has a standard way of using callbacks in async functions. The node-style expects a callback as the last argument of a function. The first parameter of the callback is an error object followed by any additional parameters. Example 4-6 shows a version of the `loadImage` function implemented in this style.

*Example 4-6. Node-style callback*

```
function loadImageNodeStyle(url, callback) {
    var image = new Image();
```

```
    image.src = url;
    image.onload = function () {
        callback(null, image);
    };
    image.onerror = function (error) {
        callback(error);
    };
}

loadImageNodeStyle('labyrinth_puzzle.png', function (err, image) {
    if (err) {
        console.log('Unable to load image');
        return;
    }
    console.log('Image loaded');
});
```

Bluebird provides a convenient function named `promisify` that wraps node-style functions with ones that return a promise, as shown in Example 4-7.

*Example 4-7. Using promisify to wrap a node-style function*

```
var loadImageWrapper = Bluebird.promisify(loadImageNodeStyle);
var promise = loadImageWrapper('computer_problems.png');

promise.then(function (image) {
    console.log('Image loaded');
}).catch(function (error) {
    console.log('Unable to load image');
});
```

The `loadImageWrapper` function accepts the same `url` argument as the original `loadImageNodeStyle` function but does not require a callback. Using `promisify` creates a callback internally and correctly wires it to a promise. If the callback receives an error the promise is rejected. Otherwise the promise is fulfilled with any additional arguments passed to the callback.

Standard promises cannot be fulfilled by more than one value. However, some node-style callbacks expect more than one value when an operation succeeds. In this case you can instruct `promisify` to fulfill the promise with an array containing all the arguments passed to the function except the error argument, which is not relevant. The array can be converted back to individual function arguments using Bluebird's `promise.spread()` method. Example 4-8 shows an example of a node-style function that provides multiple pieces of information about a user's account.

---

*Example 4-8. Converting arrays into individual arguments using promise.spread()*

```
function getAccountStatus(callback) {
    var error = null;
    var enabled = true;
    var lastLogin = new Date();

    callback(error, enabled, lastLogin);  // Callback has multiple values on success
}

var fulfillUsingAnArray = true;
var wrapperFunc = Bluebird.promisify(getAccountStatus, fulfillUsingAnArray);

// Without using spread
wrapperFunc().then(function (status) {
    var enabled = status[0];
    var lastLogin = status[1];
    // ...
});

// Using spread
wrapperFunc().spread(function (enabled, lastLogin) {
    // ...
});
```

Using `spread` in this example allows the `enabled` and `lastLogin` values to be clearly specified without the need to extract them from an array. Use `spread` to simplify the code whenever a promise is fulfilled with an array whose length and order of elements are known.

ES6 includes a feature called *destructuring* that can assign values from an array to individual variables. This feature is described in "Destructuring" on page 65.

If you want to specify the context in which the node-style function runs, you can pass the context as an argument to `promisify` or bind the context to the function before wrapping it with `promisify`, as shown in Example 4-9.

*Example 4-9. Specifying the execution context for a wrapped function*

```
var person = {
    name: 'Marie',
    introNodeStyle: function (callback) {
        var err = null;
        callback(err, 'My name is ' + this.name);
    }
};

var wrapper = Bluebird.promisify(person.introNodeStyle);
wrapper().then(function (greeting) {
    console.log('promisify without second argument: ' + greeting);
```

```
});

var wrapperWithPersonArg = Bluebird.promisify(person.introNodeStyle, person);
wrapperWithPersonArg().then(function (greeting) {
    console.log('promisify with a context argument: ' + greeting);
});

var wrapperWithBind = Bluebird.promisify(person.introNodeStyle.bind(person));
wrapperWithBind().then(function (greeting) {
    console.log('promisify using function.bind: ' + greeting);
});

// Console output:
// promisify without second argument: Hello my name is
// promisify with a context argument: Hello my name is Marie
// promisify using function.bind: Hello my name is Marie
```

Only the wrappers using a bound function or where the context was provided as a second argument include a name. All the wrappers call `person.introNodeStyle()`, which builds a string containing `this.name`. However, the first wrapper created with an undefined second argument was run in the root object scope (the window object in a web browser), which does not have a `name` property. The next wrapper specifies the context by passing it as the second argument to `promisify`. And the last one used the function's `bind` method to set the context to an object literal.

 Be careful when wrapping functions that are intended to run as methods (i.e., in the context of a certain object.) Use the function's bind or an equivalent wrapper to ensure the method is run in the expected context. Running methods in the wrong context may produce runtime errors or unexpected behavior.

## Working with Collections of Promises

Bluebird provides promise-enabled versions of the `map`, `reduce`, and `filter` methods similar to the ones available for standard JavaScript arrays. Example 4-10 shows the `filter` and `reduce` methods at work.

*Example 4-10. Using a promise-enabled filter and reduce*

```
function sumOddNumbers(numbers) {
    return numbers.filter(function removeEvenNumbers(num) {
        return num % 2 == 1;
    }).reduce(function sum(runningTotal, num) {
        return runningTotal + num;
    }, 0);
}
```

```
// Use sumOddNumbers as a synchronous function
var firstSum = sumOddNumbers([1, 2, 3, 4]);
console.log('first sum: ' + firstSum);

// Use sumOddNumbers as an async function
var promise = Bluebird.resolve([5, 6, 7, 8]);
sumOddNumbers(promise).then(function (secondSum) {
    console.log('second sum: ' + secondSum);
});

// Console output:
// first sum: 4
// second sum: 12
```

The sumOddNumbers function accepts an array of numbers and uses filter to remove any even numbers. Then reduce is used to add together the remaining values. The function works regardless of whether it is passed a standard array or a promise that an array fulfilled. These promise-enabled methods allow you to write async code that looks identical to the synchronous equivalent.

Although the synchronous and async code looks the same and produces the same result, the execution sequence may differ. The promise-enabled map, reduce, and filter methods invoke their callbacks for each value as soon as possible. When the array contains a promise, the callback is not invoked for that element until the promise is resolved. For map and filter that means the callbacks can receive values in a different order than they appear in the array. Example 4-11 shows a map passing values to the callback out of order.

*Example 4-11. Eager invocation of aggregate functions*

```
function resolveLater(value) {
    return new Bluebird(function (resolve, reject) {
        setTimeout(function () {
            resolve(value);
        }, 1000);
    });
};

var numbers = Bluebird.resolve([
    1,
    resolveLater(2),
    3
]);

console.log('Square the following numbers...');
numbers.map(function square(num) {
    console.log(num);
    return num * num;
}).then(function (result) {
```

```
    console.log('The squares of those numbers are...');
    console.log(result.join(', '));
});

// Console output:
// Square the following numbers...
// 1
// 3
// 2
// The squares of those numbers are...
// 1, 4, 9
```

When `map` is invoked it receives an array whose second element is an unresolved promise. The other two elements are numbers that are immediately passed to the the `square` callback. After fulfilling the second promise, its value is passed to `square`. Once `square` processes all the values, an array that is identical to the one that the synchronous `array.map()` function would return resolves the promise returned by `map`.

Since using `array.map()` or `Bluebird.map()` in this example produces the same `result`, it doesn't matter what order the values are passed to the callbacks. That only works as long as the callback used for `map` does not have any side effects. The `map` function is meant to convert one value to another using a callback. Adding side effects to the `map` callback conflicts with the intended use. The same thing applies to the `reduce` and `filter` functions. Avoid trouble by keeping any callbacks these functions use free from side effects.

## Manipulating Fulfillment Values

When chaining together promises to execute a series of steps, the fulfillment value of one step often provides a value needed in the next step. This progression generally works well, but sometimes multiple subsequent steps require the same value. In that case you need a way to expose the fulfillment value to additional steps.

Imagine a series of database commands that all require a connection object. If the connection is obtained through a promise in the chain it will not be available to other steps in the chain by default. You can expose the connection to other steps by assigning it to a variable in the enclosing scope, as shown in Example 4-12.

*Example 4-12. Exposing a fulfillment value using the enclosing scope*

```
var connection;  // Declare in outer scope for use in multiple functions

getConnection().then(function (con) {
    connection = con;
    return connection.insert('student', {name: 'Bobby'});
}).then(function () {
    return connection.count('students');
```

```
}).then(function (count) {
    console.log('Number of students: ' + count);
    return connection.close();
});
```

The promise chain in the example consists of three callbacks. The first callback inserts a student, the second callback fetches the number of students, and the third reports the number in the console. In order for all three callbacks to use the connection object, the fulfillment value from `getConnection` is assigned to the `connection` variable in the enclosing scope.

There are ways to expose the connection object to the other callbacks without creating a variable in the outer scope. Bluebird promises have a `return` method that returns a new promise that is resolved by the argument it is given. Example 4-13 is a revised snippet using `return` to pass the connection to the second callback.

*Example 4-13. Passing on a value using promise.return()*

```
getConnection().then(function (connection) {
    return connection
        .insert('student', {name: 'Bobby'})
        .return(connection);
}).then(function (connection) { ...
```

For this scenario you could also use the **tap** method of a Bluebird promise to get the connection object to the second callback. The **tap** method allows you to insert a callback into the promise chain while passing the fulfillment value it receives on to the next callback.

*Example 4-14. Passing on a value using promise.tap()*

```
getConnection().tap(function (connection) {
    return connection.insert('student', {name: 'Bobby'});
}).then(function (connection) { //...
```

Think of **tap** as tapping into a line without interfering with the existing flow. Use **tap** to add supplementary functions into a promise chain. A practical use for **tap** would be adding a logging statement into a promise chain, as shown in Example 4-15.

*Example 4-15. Supplementing a chain with promise.tap()*

```
function countStudents() {
    return getConnection().then(function (connection) {
        return connection.count('students');
    }).tap(function (count) {
        console.log('Number of students: ' + count);
    });
```

```
}

countStudents().then(function (count) {
    if (count > 24) console.log('Classroom has too many students');
});

// Console output:
// Number of students: 25
// Classroom has too many students
```

The call to `tap` in the `countStudents` function can be added or removed without affecting the outcome of the function.

Using `return` or `tap` masks the fulfillment value that the callback would otherwise return. That worked well in the previous examples because the results of `connection.insert()` or `console.log()` were not needed. In situations where they are needed, you can supplement the original fulfillment value with additional items in a callback by passing them in an array to `Promise.all()`, as shown in Example 4-16. Then the items in the array can be split into separate arguments of a callback using `spread`.

*Example 4-16. Passing in multiple values with Promise.all()*

```
getConnection().then(function (connection) {
    var promiseForCount = connection.count('students');
    return Promise.all([connection, promiseForCount]);
}).spread(function (connection, count) {
    console.log('Number of students: ' + count);
    return connection.close();
});
```

# Promises in jQuery

In jQuery, deferred objects represent async operations. A deferred object is like a promise whose `resolve` and `reject` functions are exposed as methods. Example 4-17 shows a `loadImage` function using a deferred object.

*Example 4-17. Simple deferred object in jQuery*

```
function loadImage(url) {
    var deferred = jQuery.Deferred();
    var img = new Image();
    img.src = url;

    img.onload = function () {
        deferred.resolve(img);
    };
```

```
    img.onerror = function (e) {
        deferred.reject(e);
    };

    return deferred;
}
```

The standard Promise API encapsulates the resolve and reject functions inside the promise. For example, if you have a promise object p, you cannot call p.resolve() or p.reject() because those functions are not attached to p. Any code that receives a reference to p can attach callbacks using p.then() or p.catch() but the code cannot control whether p gets fulfilled or rejected.

By encapsulating the resolve and reject functions inside the promise you can confidently expose the promise to other pieces of code while remaining certain the code cannot affect the fate of the promise. Without this guarantee you would have to consider all code that a promise was exposed to anytime a promise was resolved or rejected in an unexpected way.

Using deferreds does not mean you have to expose the resolve and reject methods everywhere. The deferred object also exposes a promise that can be given to any code that should not be calling resolve or reject.

Compare the two functions in Example 4-18. The first is a revised version of load Image that returns deferred.promise() and the second is the equivalent function implemented with a standard promise.

*Example 4-18. Simple deferred object in jQuery*

```
function loadImage(url) {
    var deferred = jQuery.Deferred();
    // ...
    return deferred.promise();
}

function loadImageWithoutDeferred(url) {
    return new Promise(function resolver(resolve, reject) {
        var image = new Image();
        image.src = url;
        image.onload = function () {
            resolve(image);
        };
        image.onerror = reject;
    });
}
```

The main difference between the two functions is that the function used as a deferred could throw a synchronous error while any errors thrown inside the function with the Promise constructor are caught and used to reject the promise. Promises created from jQuery deferreds do not conform to the standard ES6 Promise API or behavior. Some method names on jQuery promises differ from the spec; for example, `[jQuery Promise].fail()` is the counterpart to `[standardPromise].catch()`.

A more important difference is in handling errors in the `onFulfilled` and `onRejected` callbacks. Standard promises automatically catch any errors thrown in these callbacks and convert them into rejections. In jQuery promises, these errors bubble up the call stack as uncaught exceptions.

Also, jQuery will invoke an `onFulfilled` or `onRejected` callback synchronously if settling a promise before the callback is registered. This creates the problems with multiple execution paths described in Chapter 1.

For more differences between standard promises and the ones jQuery provides, refer to a document written by Kris Kowal titled Coming from jQuery (*http://bit.ly/kowal-jquery*).

Some developers may prefer the style of deferred objects or find them easier to understand. However, a more significant case for using a deferred is in a situation where you cannot resolve the promise in the place it is created.

Suppose you are using a web worker to perform long-running tasks. You can use promises to represent the outcome of the tasks. The code that receives the response from the web worker will resolve the promise so it needs access to the appropriate `resolve` and `reject` functions. Example 4-19 demonstrates this.

*Example 4-19. Managing web worker results with deferred objects*

```
// Contents of task.js
function onmessage(event) {
    postMessage('completed', {
        id: event.data.id,
        result: 'some computed result'
    });
}

// Contents of main.js
var worker = new Worker('task.js');
var deferreds = {};
var counter = 0;

worker.addEventListener('completed', function onCompleted(event) {
    var d = deferreds[event.data.id];
    d.resolve(event.data.result);
});
```

```
function background(task) {
    var id = counter++;
    var deferred = jQuery.Deferred();
    deferreds[id] = deferred;    // Store deferred for later resolution
    console.log('Sending task to worker: ' + task);
    worker.postMessage({
        id: id,
        task: task
    });
    return deferred.promise();   // Only expose promise to calling code
}

background('Solve for x').then(function (result) {
    console.log('The outcome is... ' + result);
}).fail(function(err) {
    console.log('Unable to complete task');
    console.log(err);
});

// Console output:
// Sending task to worker: Solve for x
// The outcome is... some calculated result
```

Example 4-19 shows the contents of two files: `tasks.js` for the web worker and `main.js` for the script that launches the worker and receives the results. The worker script is extremely simple for this example. Any time it receives a message it replies with an object containing the `id` of the original request and a hard-coded result. The `background` function in the main script returns a resolved promise once the worker sends a "completed" message for that task. Since processing the completed message occurs outside the `background` function that creates the promise, a deferred object is used to expose a `resolve` function to the `onCompleted` callback.

 For detailed information on web workers, refer to Web Workers: Multithreaded Programs in JavaScript (*http://bit.ly/webworkers_1e*) by Ido Green (O'Reilly.)

One final note for this section: if you wish to use a deferred object without jQuery, it is easy to create one using the standard Promise API, as shown in Example 4-20.

*Example 4-20. Creating a deferred object using a standard Promise constructor*

```
function Deferred() {
    var me = this;
    me.promise = new Promise(function (resolve, reject) {
        me.resolve = resolve;
```

```
        me.reject = reject;
    });
}

var d = new Deferred();
```

## Summary

Libraries offer an extended set of features for working with promises. Many of these are convenience functions that save you from mixing the plumbing with your code. This chapter covered a number of features that the Bluebird library provides, although Q and other libraries offer similar functionality and are also popular among developers. It also explained the deferred objects jQuery uses. These objects expose promises that have some significant behavioral differences compared to the ES6 standard.

# CHAPTER 5

# Error Handling

One of the biggest benefits of using promises is the way they allow you to handle errors. Async error handling with callbacks can quickly muddy a codebase with boilerplate checks in every function. Fortunately, promises allow you to replace those repetitive checks with one handler for a series of functions.

The error handling API for promises is essentially one function named `catch`. However, there are some extra things to know when using this function. For instance, it allows you to simulate an asynchronous `try/catch/finally` sequence. And it's easy to unintentionally swallow errors by forgetting to rethrow them inside a `catch` callback.

This chapter guides you through error handling in practice so you can write robust code. It includes examples using the standard Promise API as well as options the Bluebird promise library offers.

## Rejecting Promises

Basic error handling with promises was introduced in Chapter 2 using the `catch` method. You saw how a rejected promise invokes callbacks registered with `catch` (repeated in Example 5-1.)

*Example 5-1. Explicitly rejecting a promise*

```
var rejectedPromise = new Promise(function (resolve, reject) {
    reject(new Error('Arghhhh!'));     // Explicit rejection
});

rejectedPromise.catch(function (err) {
    console.log('Rejected');
    console.log(err);
});
```

```
// Console output:
// Rejected
// [Error object] { message: 'Arghhhh!' ... }
```

The `rejectedPromise` was explicitly rejected inside the callback given to the `Promise` constructor. As shown in Example 5-2, a promise is also rejected when an error is thrown inside any of the callbacks the promise invokes (i.e., any callback passed to the `Promise` constructor, then, or `catch`.)

*Example 5-2. Unhandled error rejects a promise*

```
var rejectedPromise = new Promise(function (resolve, reject) {
    throw new Error('Arghhh!');        // Implicit rejection
});
```

Any error that occurs in a function that returns a promise should be used to reject the promise instead of being thrown back to the caller. This approach allows the caller to deal with any problems that arise by attaching a `catch` handler to the returned promise instead of surrounding the call in a `try/catch` block. This can be done by wrapping code with a `Promise` constructor. Example 5-3 shows two functions to illustrate the difference between throwing a synchronous error and implicitly rejecting a promise.

*Example 5-3. Functions that return promises should not throw errors*

```
function badfunc(url) {
    var image;
    image.src = url; // Error: image is undefined
    return new Promise(function (resolve, reject) {
        image.onload = resolve;
        image.onerror = reject;
    });
}

function goodfunc(url) {
    return new Promise(function (resolve, reject) {
        var image;
        image.src = url; // Error: image is undefined
        image.onload = resolve;
        image.onload = reject;
    });
}
```

Runtime errors occur in both functions because the `image` object is never instantiated. In `badfunc` only a `try/catch` block somewhere up the stack or a global exception handler will catch the runtime error. In `goodfunc` the runtime error rejects the returned promise so the calling code can deal with it in the same way as any other problems that may arise from the operation the promise represents.

 Any error that occurs in a function that returns a promise should be used to reject the promise instead of being thrown back to the caller.

# Passing Errors

Using uncaught errors to reject promises provides an easy way to pass errors across different parts of an application and to handle them at the place of your choosing. As you saw in the last section, all the code you write inside promise callbacks is wrapped in an implicit `try` block; you just need to provide the `catch`. When presented with a chain of promises, add a `catch` wherever it is helpful to deal with a rejection. Although you could add a `catch` handler to every promise in a chain, it is generally practical to use a single handler at the end of the chain.

Where does a promise chain end? It's common for a single function to contain a chain of several promises that a series of calls to `then` defines. However, the chain may not end there. Promise chains are frequently extended across functions as each caller appends a promise to the tail.

Consider an async function that opens a database connection, runs a query, and returns a promise that is fulfilled with the resulting data. The function returns the last promise in the chain but the calling function will add to that chain so it can do something with the results, as shown in Example 5-4. The pattern continues as the new tail is returned to the next calling function, as described in "The Async Ripple Effect" on page 25.

*Example 5-4. Promise chains built across functions*

```
var db = {
  connect: function () {/*...*/};
  query: function () {/*...*/};
};

function getReportData() {
    return db.connect().then(function (connection) {
        return db.query(connection, 'select report data');
    });
}

getReportData().then(function (data) {
    data.sort();
    console.log(data);
```

```
}).catch(function (err) {
    console.log('Unable to show data');
});
```

In this code the promise chain ends at the bottom of the script after the data is sorted and written to the console. The end of the chain has a catch function to handle any problems that may occur along the way. Since the chain does not terminate in getReportData, it is not necessary to include a catch function there. However, you may wish to include one to put some logging statements close to the source of a potential error.

The catch function returns a new promise similar to then, but the promise that catch returns is only rejected if the callback throws an error. In other words, you must explicitly rethrow an error inside a catch callback if you want the rejection to continue propagating through the promise chain. Example 5-5 shows an updated version of getReportData that includes a handler to log errors.

*Example 5-5. Logging and rethrowing an error*

```
function getReportData() {
    return db.connect().then(function (connection) {
        return db.query(connection, 'select something');
    }).catch(function (err) {
        console.log('An error occurred while getting the data');
        if (err && err.message) console.log(err.message);
        throw err; // Must re-throw if you want the rejection to propagate further
    });
}
```

If db.connect() or db.query() return promises that are rejected and the catch callback in getData does not include the throw statement, then getData will always return a resolved promise. In this case a runtime error would occur when data.sort() is called because the value of data would be undefined.

# Unhandled Rejections

It's easy to forget to add a catch handler to your promise chain. You may start by writing code for the happy path and consider your work done once things behave as expected. Missing a catch handler can be difficult to troubleshoot because the rejected promise sits silently somewhere in your codebase, as opposed to traditional runtime errors that are immediately written to the console and may bring your application to a halt.

Bluebird implements one solution to this problem. After the rejection of a bluebird promise, the console displays the reason if no catch handlers are registered for the rejection by the time the event loop turns twice, as shown in Example 5-6. Waiting for two turns of the loop gives your code time to deal with a rejected promise, which reduces the chance of a handled rejection showing up in the console.

*Example 5-6. Bluebird reporting an unhandled rejection*

```
Bluebird.reject('No one listens to turtle');

// Console output:
// Possibly unhandled Error: No one listens to turtle
//     at Function.Promise$Reject ...
```

The developer tools in your web browser may also report unhandled rejections. At the time this book was written, Chrome and Mozilla Firefox both did this but in slightly different ways. Chrome logged unhandled rejections immediately whereas Firefox waited until garbage collection occurred. The Firefox approach introduces a delay but eliminates false positives (i.e., showing a rejection that is eventually handled.)

# Implementing try/catch/finally

A try/catch/finally flow allows you to run some code, handle any exceptions that the code throws, and then run some final code regardless of whether an exception occurred. To see why this is useful, first consider the following function in Example 5-7, which fetches some data and uses the performance.now() Web API to log the amount of time taken.

*Example 5-7. A try/catch block*

```
function getData() {
    var timestamp = performance.now();
    try {
        // Fetch data
        // ...
    } catch (err) {
        // Deal with any errors that arise
        // ...
    }
    console.log('getData() took ' + (performance.now() - timestamp));
}
```

The log statement always runs regardless of whether an error occurs inside the try block because catch handles any error. Unfortunately this approach swallows the errors, so the code that calls getData never knows when an error occurs. In order to inform the calling code, the catch block needs to rethrow the error, but that will bypass the log statement. That's where the finally block comes in.

Example 5-8 is an example of a traditional try/catch/finally block.

*Example 5-8. A traditional try/catch/finally block*

```
function getData() {
    var timestamp = performance.now();
    try {
        // Fetch data
        // ...
    } catch (err) {
        // Bubble error up to code that called this function
        throw err;
    } finally {
        // Log time taken regardless of whether the preceding code throws an error
        console.log('getData() took ' + (performance.now() - timestamp));
    }
}


// Console output:
// getData() took 0.030000000158906914
```

You can create an asynchronous try/catch/finally block using promises. We've already seen how any errors thrown within a promise chain are sent to the next catch callback in the chain, similar to using traditional try/catch blocks. To implement the finally portion, follow the call to catch with then and do not rethrow the error provided to catch, as shown in Example 5-9.

*Example 5-9. Use catch/then to mimic catch/finally*

```
function getData() {
    var dataPromise;
    var timestamp = performance.now();

    dataPromise = new Promise(function (resolve, reject) {
        // ...
        throw new Error('Unexpected problem');
    });

    dataPromise.catch(function (err) {
        // Do not rethrow error
    }).then(function () {
        // Simulates finally block
        console.log('Data fetch took ' + (performance.now() - timestamp));
    });

    // Return data promise instead of catch/then tail to propagate rejection
    return dataPromise;
}
```

The code in Example 5-9 creates a chain of three promises: the `dataPromise`, the promise returned by `catch`, and the promise returned by `then`. The promise returned by `catch` is always fulfilled because no error is thrown inside the callback given to `catch`. That promise executes the callback passed to `then`, which contains the same code that would have been placed in a finally block.

Some promise libraries, including Bluebird, implement a `promise.finally()` method for convenience. This method runs regardless of whether the promise is fulfilled or rejected and returns a promise that is settled in the same way. Example 5-10 shows a revised version of `getData` using `bluebirdPromise.finally()`.

*Example 5-10. Bluebird's promise.finally()*

```
function getData() {
    var timestamp = performance.now();

    return new Bluebird(function (resolve, reject) {
        // ...
        throw new Error('Unexpected problem');
    }).finally(function () {
        console.log('Data fetch took ' + (performance.now() - timestamp));
    });
}
```

The revised code is simpler because `bluebirdPromise.finally()` can remove the explicit promise variable and `catch` function needed to mimic a finally block using the standard Promise API.

# Using the Call Stack

It is often helpful to examine the call stack when troubleshooting code because it answers the question *How did I get here?* Whenever a function is invoked, the line that called the function is added to the stack. When an error occurs, the stack contains the trail of calls that shows how the machine arrived at that point. A typical view of the stack lists the name of each function in the trail and the line number of the code that called the next function.

The JavaScript call stack starts with whatever code the runtime inside the current turn of the event loop invoked. The stack continues to grow as that code calls another function, which in turn calls another function, etc. As each function returns, it is removed from the stack until the stack is empty, at which point the event loop turns again.

Example 5-11 shows a function that is called whenever clicking the mouse or pressing a key along with the associated call stack.

*Example 5-11. Sample call stack*

```
function echo(text) {
    console.log(text);
    throw Error('oops');

    // Example of call stack for error when triggered by a mouse click:
    // echo (line:3)
    // showRandomNumber (line:12)
    // handleClick (line:16)
}

function showRandomNumber() {
    echo(Math.random());
}

document.addEventListener('click', function handleClick() {
    showRandomNumber();
});

document.addEventListener('keypress', function handleKeypress() {
    showRandomNumber();
});
```

The call stack shows you whether `handleClick` or `handleKeypress` triggered the `echo` function. In a larger program, knowing the execution path can go a long way toward finding the cause of a problem.

Unfortunately, the current call stack is generally not as helpful when promises are involved. In Example 5-12, we have revised Example 5-11 to call the echo function using `promise.then()`. As a result, the call stack inside `echo` no longer includes `handleClick` or `showRandomNumber`.

*Example 5-12. Promise callback breaks up the call stack*

```
function echo(text) {
    console.log(text);
    throw new Error('oops');

    // Example of call stack for error when invoked as a callback for a promise
    // echo (line:3)
}

function showRandomNumber() {
    // Invoking echo as a promise callback
    var p = Promise.resolve(Math.random());
    p.then(echo).catch(function (error) {
        console.log(error.stack)
    });
}
```

```
document.addEventListener('click', function handleClick() {
    showRandomNumber();
});

document.addEventListener('keypress', function handleKeypress() {
    showRandomNumber();
});
```

Why does using a promise callback appear to truncate the stack when compared to the earlier example? Remember that a promise invokes each callback in a separate turn of the event loop. At the beginning of each turn the stack is empty, so none of the functions called in previous turns appear in the stack when the error occurs.

Losing the stack between each callback makes troubleshooting harder. The problem is not unique to promises; it exists for any asynchronous callbacks. However, it can be a frequent source of frustration when using promises. To address this problem in the debugger, the Chrome team added an option to show the stack across turns of the event loop. Now you can see a stack that is stitched together at the points where asynchronous calls are made. A dedicated panel for debugging promises in the Chrome developer tools is also in the works. This is a huge help and other browsers may offer a similar feature by the time you read this.

You may also record errors that occur while people are using your software in the wild. When that happens, you don't have the luxury of opening the debugger and looking at the stack. Developers have found clever ways to capture the async call stack using multiple Error objects. This is problematic because browsers expose the call stack for errors in different ways and it can degrade application performance. You can configure Bluebird to capture and report the stack trace across turns of the event loop by calling `Bluebird.longStackTraces()`. Keep in mind the impact on performance before enabling this option in the production version of your application.

## Summary

Handling errors in asynchronous code cannot be done with traditional `try/catch` blocks. Fortunately, promises have a `catch` method for handling asynchronous errors. Although the method is a powerful tool for handling problems that occur deep within your code, you must use it properly to avoid silently swallowing errors. In addition to the functionality that the standard Promise API provides, libraries such as Bluebird offer extra error handling features. This includes the ability to report unhandled rejections and to capture the call stack across multiple turns of the event loop.

# CHAPTER 6

# Combining ECMAScript 6 Features with Promises

ECMAScript 6 has a number of language features that complement promises. This chapter shows how destructuring, arrow functions, iterators, and generators simplify your promise-related code. However, this is not a full explanation of these features or ES6. It is merely a starting point for taking advantage of ES6 in your code.

The new syntax that these features require causes errors in JavaScript environments that do not support them. Unlike the Promise API that is unobtrusively polyfilled, code that uses the new syntax must be modified in order to run in older environments. You can automate the modification by transpiling the code into something equivalent that runs in older environments. However, multiple JavaScript environments such as Google Chrome and Mozilla Firefox already support some of these features, such as generators. The ECMAScript 6 compatibility table (*http://bit.ly/compatibility_table*) maintained by Juriy Zaytsev (a.k.a. kangax) on GitHub is a good place to see which ES6 features are available on your target platform.

## Destructuring

Destructuring provides a syntax for extracting values from arrays or objects into individual variables. Instead of writing individual assignment statements for each variable, destructuring allows you to assign the values for multiple variables in a single statement. Examples 6-1 and 6-2 present destructuring using an array and an object.

*Example 6-1. Array destructuring*

```
var numbers = [10, 20];
var [n1, n2] = numbers;    // destructuring
```

```
console.log(n1);            // 10
console.log(n2);            // 20
```

*Example 6-2. Object destructuring*

```
var position = {x: 50, y: 100};
var {x, y} = position;           // destructuring
console.log(x);                  // 50
console.log(y);                  // 100
```

The destructuring syntax can also be used when declaring function parameters. In Chapter 3, an example from the WHATWG Streams specification (*http://bit.ly/whatwg_streams*) used a promise fulfilled with an object containing two properties: value and done. Example 6-3 is a comparison of how the onFulfilled callback can be written with destructuring.

*Example 6-3. Object destructuring with function parameters*

```
// Without destructuring
reader.read().then(function (result) {
    // ... Use result.value and result.done
});

// Using destructuring
reader.read().then(function ({value, done}) {
    // ... Use done and value directly
});
```

Array destructuring also works in function parameters. Example 4-16 mapped values from an array to parameters called enabled and lastLogin using blue birdPromise.spread(). Example 6-4 shows the equivalent code using destructuring.

*Example 6-4. Array destructuring with function parameters*

```
// Without destructuring
getAccountStatus().then(function (status) {
    var enabled = status[0];
    var lastLogin = status[1];
    // ...
});

// Using destructuring
getAccountStatus().then(function ([enabled, lastLogin]) {
    // ... Use enabled and lastLogin directly
});
```

Array destructuring is also useful for handling the fulfillment value of Promise.all(), as seen in Example 6-5.

*Example 6-5. Destructuring the fulfillment value from Promise.all()*

```
Promise.all([promise1, promise2]).then(function ([result1, result2]) {
    // ...
});
```

# Arrow Functions

The arrow function syntax is like shorthand for declaring anonymous functions. In lieu of a full explanation of this new syntax, let's create a simple example using an arrow function and then apply it to promises.

Arrow functions are useful for declaring callbacks that you would typically write as inline functions. In "Parallel Execution" on page 28, an array of bank and credit card accounts was mapped to requests for their current balance using the code in Example 6-6.

*Example 6-6. Using array.map() with an inline callback*

```
requests = accounts.forEach(function (account) {
    return getBalance(account);
});
```

The code in Example 6-6 can be rewritten as it appears in Example 6-7 using an arrow function.

*Example 6-7. Using array.map() with an arrow function*

```
requests = accounts.map(account => getBalance(account));
```

The new syntax always omits the `function` keyword. When there is only one parameter, the parentheses around the parameter may also be dropped. And when the body of the function consists of a single return statement, the enclosing braces and the word `return` can be left out as well. The noise created by the traditional function syntax is stripped away, leaving a concise piece of code.

Now let's use the arrow function syntax in a chain of promises. The section "Functional Composition" on page 36 used the code in Example 6-8 to create an image processing pipeline.

*Example 6-8. Concise pipeline (repeated from earlier chapter)*

```
function processImage(image) {
    // Image is always last parameter preceded by any configuration parameters
    var customScaleToFit = scaleToFit.bind(null, 300, 450);
    var customWatermark = watermark.bind(null, 'The Real Estate Company');
```

```
    return Promise.resolve(image)
        .then(customScaleToFit)
        .then(customWatermark)
        .then(grayscale);
}
```

Example 6-9 shows a version of the pipeline using arrow functions.

*Example 6-9. Concise pipeline with arrow functions*

```
function processImage(image) {
    return Promise.resolve(image)
        .then(image => scaleToFit(300, 450, image))
        .then(image => watermark('The Real Estate Company', image))
        .then(image => grayscale(image))
        .then(({src}) => console.log('Processing completed for ' + src));
}
```

This version also includes a logging function at the end of the chain that uses destructuring to directly access the src property of the image.

Using arrow functions allows you to create one-line callbacks for each of the steps in the pipeline without creating prebound functions at the top of processImage. This is just another way to accomplish the same thing as the previous version of process Image; the implementation style is a matter of preference.

# Iterables and Iterators

ES6 introduces the ability to iterate through multiple items that an object provides. This is similar to walking through the items in an array using an index or through the properties of an object using for…in. However, iterators differ from both of these because they allow any object to provide an arbitrary series of items as opposed to one that is based on the object's keys. For instance, an object called linkedlist could provide all the items in the list and an object called tree could expose all of its nodes.

One can access the items through a combination of two interfaces (also known as protocols), which are predefined sets of functions with specific names and behaviors. Objects that expose a series of items are known as iterables. These objects provide an iterator that exposes one item at a time and indicates when the series is exhausted. Thus the two interfaces are named *iterable* and *iterator*.

Objects that want to expose a series of items can implement the iterable interface by defining a function whose name is the value of Symbol.iterator, that is, object[Symbol.iterator] = function () {…}. This function should return an object with the iterator interface.

The iterator interface has one method named next. The method returns an object with two properties named value and done. The value represents the current item in the iteration and the done property is a flag to indicate when there are no more values available from the iterator.

Arrays are iterables so they contain the Symbol.iterator method, as shown in Example 6-10.

*Example 6-10. Using the iterable interface of an array*

```
var array = [1, 2];
var iterator = array[Symbol.iterator]();

iterator.next();    // {value: 1, done: false}
iterator.next();    // {value: 2, done: false}
iterator.next();    // {value: undefined, done: true}
```

How do iterables relate to promises? The Promise.all() and Promise.race() functions both accept iterables. Although an array is probably the most common type of iterable you would use with these functions, other options are available. For instance, the Set datatype in ES6 is also an iterable. A set is a collection of items that does not contain duplicates. You can pass a set to Promise.all() or you can use a custom iterable by implementing the interface on an object you define.

In addition to working with Promise.all() and Promise.race(), iterators work closely with ES6 generators, as described in the next section.

# Generators

ES6 includes a feature called *generators* that allows you to write async code that looks synchronous. Generators are not easy to explain in a few sentences. Let's begin with the end in mind by showing the style of async code that can be written when you combine promises and generators. Then we'll work through the individual concepts required to understand that code.

## Synchronous Style

Let's use the async loadImage function in Example 6-11 as a starting point for the discussion.

*Example 6-11. Managing asynchronous image loading using a promise*

```
loadImage('thesis_defense.png').then(function (img) {
    document.body.appendChild(img);
}).catch(function (e) {
    console.log('Error occurred while loading image');
```

```
        console.log(e);
});
```

Callbacks passed to then and catch handle the outcome of loadImage because load
Image returns a promise. If the image was loaded synchronously the calling code
could be written as shown in Example 6-12.

*Example 6-12. Hypothetical use of loadImage as a synchronous function*

```
try {
    var img = loadImage('thesis_defense.png');
    document.body.appendChild(img);
} catch (err) {
    console.log('Error occured while loading the image');
    console.log(err);
}
```

The synchronous version of loadImage returns the image for immediate use and a
traditional try/catch block helps perform error handling. When you combine generators and promises you can write code that looks like this even though the functions
being called are asynchronous. Example 6-13 uses the asynchronous version of load
Image with a generator.

*Example 6-13. Using a promise with code that looks synchronous*

```
async(function* () {
    try {
        var img = yield loadImage('thesis_defense.png');
        document.body.appendChild(img);
    } catch (err) {
        console.log('Error occurred while loading the image');
        console.log(err);
    }
})();
```

Ignoring the first line for a moment, we see that the remaining code is identical to the
synchronous equivalent except for one yield keyword added before the call to load
Image. This simple change allows you to write async code in this fashion. The rest of
the chapter explains how that is possible.

## Generators and Iterators

A generator is a special type of function that can pause its execution to pass values
back to its caller and later resume executing where it left off. This ability is useful for
generating a series of values. The Fibonacci sequence can be used as an example.
Without using generators it can be computed as shown in Example 6-14.

*Example 6-14. Computing a series of values without using a generator*

```
var a = 0;
var b = 1;

function fib() {
    b = a + b;
    a = b - a;
    return b;
}

var i;
for (i = 0; i < 5; i++) console.log(fib());

// Console output:
// 1
// 2
// 3
// 5
// 8
```

The fib function tracks the last two values used in the sequence and adds them together every time it is called to calculate the next value. Example 6-15 shows the equivalent code using a generator.

*Example 6-15. Computing a series of values using a generator*

```
function* fib() {
    var a = 0;
    var b = 1;
    while (true) {
        yield a + b;
        b = a + b;
        a = b - a;
    }
}

var i;
var result;
var iterator = fib();
for (i = 0; i < 5; i++) {
    result = iterator.next();
    console.log(result.value);
}
```

```
// Console output is identical to the previous example
```

The fib function is now a generator, which is indicated by adding the * at the end of the function keyword. When the generator is called, the JavaScript engine does not start running the code inside fib as it would with a normal function. Instead the call to `fib` returns an iterator. The iterator is used to pause and resume execution of the generator and pass values between the generator and the calling code.

The code inside `fib` starts running the first time `iterator.next()` is called. Execution continues until the `yield` keyword. At that point the function pauses and sends the result of the `yield` expression back to the calling code as the return value of `iterator.next()`. The result is an object that provides the outcome of the `yield` statement in a property named `value`.

When `iterator.next()` is called again the code inside `fib` resumes execution on the line after the `yield` statement. The values of `a` and `b` are updated and the next iteration of the `while` loop hits the yield statement, which repeats the pause and send behavior for another number in the sequence.

A generator may contain multiple `yield` statements but in this case it has one `yield` placed inside an infinite `while` loop. The loop allows the iterator to provide an indefinite amount of Fibonacci numbers. In the previous example the calling code stopped making requests after five values.

Example 6-15 introduced three concepts: the generator declaration syntax, the iterator, and the `yield` keyword. That's a lot to comprehend at once but all three are necessary to create a basic example. Consider reviewing the previous snippet and explanation until you are comfortable with these concepts.

## Sending Values to a Generator

Not only can values be passed from the generator back to the calling code, they can also be passed from the calling code into the generator. The `iterator.next()` method accepts a parameter that is used as a result of the `yield` expression inside the generator. Example 6-16 demonstrates passing a value into the generator. In this case a function counts things one at a time by default but can be adjusted to count in any increment.

*Example 6-16. Passing values into the generator*

```
function* counter() {
    var count = 0;
    var increment = 1;
    while (true) {
        count = count + increment;
        increment = (yield count) || increment;
    }
}

var iterator = counter();
console.log(iterator.next().value);     // 1
console.log(iterator.next().value);     // 2
```

```
console.log(iterator.next().value);      // 3
console.log(iterator.next(10).value);    // 13 <- Start counting by 10
console.log(iterator.next().value);      // 23
console.log(iterator.next().value);      // 33
```

The fourth call to `iterator.next()` sets the `increment` value to 10. All the other calls to `iterator.next()` pass a value of `undefined` by not providing an explicit argument.

A generator can also declare parameters similar to a traditional function. The values for these parameters are set when the iterator is created and they may act as a configuration for the iterator. Example 6-17 is a revised version of the counter whose initial increment can be set by a parameter.

*Example 6-17. Configuring an iterator with an initial parameter*

```
function* counter(increment) {
    var count = 0;
    increment = increment || 1;
    while (true) {
        count = count + increment;
        increment = (yield count) || increment;
    }
}

var evens = counter(2);
console.log('Even numbers');         // Even numbers
console.log(evens.next().value);     // 2
console.log(evens.next().value);     // 4
console.log(evens.next().value);     // 6

var fives = counter(5);
console.log('Count by fives');       // Count by fives
console.log(fives.next().value);     // 5
console.log(fives.next().value);     // 10
console.log(fives.next().value);     // 15
```

Two iterators are created from `counter` with different configurations. Creating iterators from a generator is similar to creating objects from a constructor function. Each iterator maintains its own state to apply general code, such as counting in predefined increments, to the specific cases of counting in even numbers or counting by fives.

We've discussed how values can be passed to generators using the initial parameters and as an argument to `iterator.next()`. However, there are two cases where the argument to `iterator.next()` is ignored. The argument is always ignored the first time `iterator.next()` is called. Example 6-18 shows the value being ignored followed by an explanation of why it happens.

*Example 6-18. The parameter in the first call to iterator.next() is always ignored*

```
// Same function* counter as previous example
function* counter(increment) {
    var count = 0;
    increment = increment || 1;
    while (true) {
        count = count + increment;
        increment = (yield count) || increment;
    }
}
```

```
var iterator = counter(5);          //       <- Initial increment is 5
console.log(iterator.next(3).value); // 5    <- 3 is ignored
console.log(iterator.next().value);  // 10
console.log(iterator.next(200).value); // 210 <- Increment by 200
console.log(iterator.next().value);  // 410
```

The number 3 passed in the first call to `iterator.next()` has no effect in the code because the generator syntax and API do not provide a way to receive this value. All values that the `next` method passes to the generator are received when the code resumes after a `yield` statement as `val = yield`. However, the first call to `next` does not resume the function from a paused state. The first call starts the initial execution of the function and there is no mechanism for receiving a value at that point. In a traditional function the parameters serve that purpose but in a generator the call that creates the iterator sets the parameter values.

The other case where an argument to `iterator.next()` is ignored is after the function returns. All the previous examples contain infinite loops that paused the function to send back a value. When a generator function returns from execution in the traditional sense as opposed to pausing on yield, there is no way to receive more data from the iterator. Example 6-19 is a generator that returns after filtering objects in an array.

*Example 6-19. Finite iterations*

```
function* match(objects, propname, value) {
    var i;
    var obj;
    for (i = 0; i < objects.length; i++) {
        obj = objects[i];
        if (obj[propname] === value) yield obj;
    };
}

var animals = [
    { type: 'bird', legs: 2 },
    { type: 'cat', legs: 4 },
    { type: 'dog', legs: 4 },
    { type: 'spider', legs: 8 }
```

```
];

var iterator = match(animals, 'legs', 4);
console.log(iterator.next().value.type); // value is an animal
console.log(iterator.next().value.type); // value is an animal
console.log(iterator.next().value);      // value is undefined

// Console output:
// cat
// dog
// undefined
```

The match generator accepts an array of objects along with a property name and value used to filter the objects. Any object with a matching property and value is yielded back to the calling code. After checking all the objects, the function returns. Any value returned by the function is used in the final result. And any result objects that next returns after that point have their value property set as undefined.

The result that next returns also exposes a done property to indicate when the iterator has finished executing. The property is useful for looping through the results as shown in Example 6-20.

*Example 6-20. Looping through iterations*

```
// Substitute for iterator and console.log in previous example
iterator = match(animals, 'legs', 4);
while ((result = iterator.next()).done !== true) {
    console.log(result.value.type);
}

// Console output:
// cat
// dog
```

Each turn of the while loop assigns the next iteration result to an object and checks the done flag. This is a vast improvement over hardcoding for the expected number of results, but there is a more elegant way to write this loop. A new for...of construct, as shown in Example 6-21, allows you to implicitly manage the iterator. Use for...of if you are dealing with a finite number of iterations and do not need to pass values back to the generator.

*Example 6-21. Using an implicit iterator created by for...of*

```
// Better substitute for iterator and loop
for (animal of match(animals, 'legs', 4)) {
    console.log(animal.type);
}
```

# Sending Errors to a Generator

An iterator can cause an error to be thrown when execution resumes inside a generator. Example 6-22 is a contrived scenario to demonstrate the functionality. The example prints *hello* in a series of languages that a generator provides. An error is thrown when there is no translation available for the language. Note the call to iterator.throw() at the bottom of the example.

*Example 6-22. Throwing errors with the iterator*

```
function* languages() {
    try {
        yield 'English';
        yield 'French';
        yield 'German';
        yield 'Spanish';
    } catch (error) {
        console.log(error.message);
    }
}

var greetings = {
    English: 'Hello',
    French: 'Bonjour',
    Spanish: 'Hola'
};
var iterator = languages();
var result;
var word;
while ((result = iterator.next()).done !== true) {
    word = greetings[result.value];
    if (word) console.log(word);
    else iterator.throw(Error('Missing translation for ' + result.value));
}

// Console output:
// Hello
// Bonjour
// Missing translation for German
```

When the iterator yields "German" there is no translation found for that language so an error is sent to the generator using iterator.throw(). The error is thrown inside the generator where the yield \'German' expression is evaluated. The yield \'Spanish' statement is skipped, as the error immediately falls to the catch block. Although sending an error back to the generator in this example is not useful, this ability is needed to write synchronous-looking code using promises and generators.

## Practical Application

Now let's revisit Example 6-13 from "Synchronous Style" on page 69 to see how it works. Example 6-23 repeats the code here for convenience.

*Example 6-23. Using a promise with code that looks synchronous (repeated from earlier)*

```
async(function* () {
    try {
        var img = yield loadImage('thesis_defense.png');
        document.body.appendChild(img);
    } catch (err) {
        console.log('caught in async routine');
        console.log(err);
    }
})();
```

The `loadImage` function is called in the body of a generator. Although `loadImage` returns a promise, the `yield` statement inside the generator returns the fulfillment value of that promise: an image object in this case. How is that possible? Instead of directly creating an iterator from the generator and invoking `iterator.next()`, the generator is passed to `async`, which returns a wrapper function. When the wrapper is invoked it intercepts any promise that the generator yields and waits for it to settle. Once the promise is fulfilled its value is passed into the generator. If the promise is rejected its rejection reason is thrown inside the generator.

There are several ways to implement the `async` function. Example 6-24 shows one way based on code written by Forbes Lindesay on promisejs.org (*https://www.promis ejs.org/generators/*).

*Example 6-24. Sample async wrapper*

```
function async(generator) {
    return function () {
        var iterator = generator.apply(this, arguments);

        function handle(result) {
            if (result.done) return Promise.resolve(result.value);

            return Promise.resolve(result.value).then(function (res) {
                return handle(iterator.next(res));
            }, function (err) {
                return handle(iterator.throw(err));
            });
        }

        try {
            return handle(iterator.next());
```

```
        } catch (ex) {
            return Promise.reject(ex);
        }
    };
}
```

The wrapper function also returns a promise that the return value of the generator fulfills or any unhandled error rejects. This behavior is identical to any callback registered with `promise.then()` or `promise.catch()`. If you prefer handling errors with `promise.catch` instead of traditional `try/catch` blocks, you can attach a `catch` to the promise that the `async` wrapper returns, as shown in Example 6-25.

*Example 6-25. Replacing try/catch with promise.catch()*

```
async(function* () {
    var img = yield loadImage('thesis_defense.png');
    document.body.appendChild(img);
})().catch(function (err) {
    console.log('caught in rejection handler');
    console.log(err);
});
```

Some promise libraries provide a function similar to `async`, such as `Q.async()` and `Bluebird.coroutine()`. Using these functions to wrap a single call to a promise is probably overkill, but this style is useful when dealing with multiple asynchronous steps in a single function because you can replace all the `promise.then()` callbacks with synchronous return values.

There is a plan to introduce `async` and `await` keywords in ECMAScript 7, as shown in Example 6-26, that will remove the need for the `async(generator)` pattern described in this section.

*Example 6-26. Using async and await as proposed in ES7*

```
async function () {
    try {
        var img = await loadImage('thesis_defense.png');
        document.body.appendChild(img);
    } catch (err) {
        console.log('caught in rejection handler');
        console.log(err);
    }
});
```

The proposed syntax allows you to declare an async function instead of using a generator. Since the function is not a generator, the `yield` keyword is replaced with `await`. All other parts of the code are identical and this function behaves the same as its ES6 counterpart. The purpose is to remove the burden of supplying a boilerplate async function.

## Summary

This chapter showed how some of the new language features in ES6 can be used with promises. These features all allow you to write less code to accomplish the same outcome. We began with simplifying access to fulfillment values using destructuring, followed by concise callback declarations using arrow functions. And we concluded with how iterators and generators can be used to treat async functions that return promises as synchronous code.

This chapter also concludes the book. We started with the fundamentals of asynchronous programming in JavaScript and worked through the core concepts in Promises and how to utilize them in a wide variety of scenarios. At this point you should be prepared to confidently manage async tasks with Promises, absorb new promise-based APIs such as Service Workers (*http://bit.ly/service_workers/*) or Streams (*http://bit.ly/whatwg_streams*), and even create your own promise-based API.

# Index

(see also error propagation)
    unhandled, 58
    versus thrown errors, 56
resolved promises, 23, 27
run to completion, 6-10
runtime errors, 56

## S

sequential execution, 30-35
    with loops, 32-33
    with recursion, 33-34
set, 69
settled promises, 16
states, 15-18
substitute promises, 27

## T

then, 22

(see also catch/then)
then and catch, 12, 70
thenable contracts, 40
try/catch, 56, 78
try/catch/finally blocks, 59-61

## U

unhandled rejections, 58

## V

verbose pipeline, 36

## W

wrapping Node.js functions, 43-46

## Y

yield, 70-72

## About the Author

**Daniel Parker** is a software developer focused on web and mobile applications. He writes JavaScript for Evernote in Austin, Texas, and is the organizer of the Austin Google Developer Group.

## Colophon

The animal on the cover of *JavaScript with Promises* is a white-crested helmetshrike (*Prionops plumatus*). These birds are widespread and common throughout southern Africa, inhabiting tropical and subtropical woodlands, savanna, and shrubland. The name comes from ornamental frills of white feathers that sprout from the forehead.

Helmetshrikes are medium-sized birds, ranging from 19 to 25 centimeters and weighing between 25 to 37 grams. Their plumage is black, white, and gray, with a distinctive white stripe on the wings. Other distinctive features include a hooked beak and bright yellow eyes. They primarily feed on caterpillars, moths, crickets, and grasshoppers, in addition to small lizards and fruit.

Helmetshrikes are extremely sociable birds, rarely seen unaccompanied. They are also cooperative breeders, forming small groups that assist a single dominant mating pair in nesting duties. The breeding pair selects the nesting site, but all members help build the nest, incubate the eggs, and feed and protect the nestlings. Nests are made of bark and held together with cobwebs, which serves for camouflage. The helmetshrike's head feathers are advantageous in this regard, enabling it to pick up spiderwebs for nest construction.

Many of the animals on O'Reilly covers are endangered; all of them are important to the world. To learn more about how you can help, go to *animals.oreilly.com*.

The cover image is from loose plates (original source unknown). The cover fonts are URW Typewriter and Guardian Sans. The text font is Adobe Minion Pro; the heading font is Adobe Myriad Condensed; and the code font is Dalton Maag's Ubuntu Mono.

# Get even more for your money.

## Join the O'Reilly Community, and register the O'Reilly books you own. It's free, and you'll get:

- $4.99 ebook upgrade offer
- 40% upgrade offer on O'Reilly print books
- Membership discounts on books and events
- Free lifetime updates to ebooks and videos
- Multiple ebook formats, DRM FREE
- Participation in the O'Reilly community
- Newsletters
- Account management
- 100% Satisfaction Guarantee

### Signing up is easy:

1. Go to: oreilly.com/go/register
2. Create an O'Reilly login.
3. Provide your address.
4. Register your books.

Note: English-language books only

**To order books online:**
oreilly.com/store

**For questions about products or an order:**
orders@oreilly.com

**To sign up to get topic-specific email announcements and/or news about upcoming books, conferences, special offers, and new technologies:**
elists@oreilly.com

**For technical questions about book content:**
booktech@oreilly.com

**To submit new book proposals to our editors:**
proposals@oreilly.com

**O'Reilly books are available in multiple DRM-free ebook formats. For more information:**
oreilly.com/ebooks